# BASIL
# THYME
# CORIANDER
## and Other Herbs

# BASIL
# THYME
# CORIANDER
## and Other Herbs

Jean-Paul Grappe

Fitzhenry & Whiteside

First published in English by Fitzhenry & Whiteside in 2014

Originally published in French under the title *Basilic, thym, coriandre et autres herbes...* © 2003, Les Editions de L'Homme, division du Groupe Sogides Inc. (Montréal, Québec, Canada)

www.fitzhenry.ca          godwit@fitzhenry.ca

Fitzhenry & Whiteside acknowledges with thanks the Canada Council for the Arts, and the Ontario Arts Council for their support of our publishing program. We acknowledge the financial support of the Government of Canada through the Canada Book Fund (CBF) for our publishing activities.

Translator: Marcella Walton
Designer: Daniel Choi

Library and Archives Canada Cataloguing in Publication
Grappe, Jean-Paul
[Basilic, thym, coriandre et autres herbes.  English]
     Basil, thyme, coriander & other herbs / Jean-Paul Grappe.
Translation of: Basilic, thym, coriandre et autres herbes.
ISBN 978-1-55455-288-7 (pbk.)
     1. Cooking (Herbs).  2. Cooking (Basil).  3. Cooking (Thyme).
4. Cooking (Coriander).  5. Cookbooks.  I. Title.  II. Titre: Basilic, thym, coriandre et autres herbes.  English.
TX819.H4G7213 2014          641.6'57          C2013-908194-1

Publisher Cataloging-in-Publication Data  (U.S.)
Basil, Thyme, Coriander and Other Herbs
ISBN 978-1-55455-288-7
Data available on file

Printed and bound by Sheck Wah Tong Printing Press Ltd. in Hong Kong, China
10 9 8 7 6 5 4 3 2 1

The team: Pierre Beauchemin, Colombe St. Pierre, Jean-Paul Grappe and Julien Bartoluci

To Christine

# Preface

Since the dawn of cuisine, the infinite diversity of plants has fascinated us, ever since we realized that plants were a source of food as well as a source of life. Not only were plants an important element of cooking, but they could also be used to make medicines. From the time our Neanderthal ancestors began making flint (Mousterian) tools, they marvelled at the blossoming tundra that came to life each spring. Thousands of years later, the Greeks recognized the importance of plants and their many uses. By the 18th century, how many people were involved in horticulture and botany, so venerated by Rousseau? Today, along paths, by the side of small country roads or forest trails, we see a yearly renewal of plant life. Fiddleheads, wild leeks, lovage, creeping thyme, mustard, wild salsify, vegetables, and herbs grow in abundance to the delight of foragers.

Explorers searching for the spice route brought seeds from countries with warmer climates. Today, many of us have small herb gardens in our yards. We take time each morning to smell the rosemary, basil, marjoram, coriander, tarragon, and many others. I met Jean-Paul Grappe about twenty years ago when I began growing aromatic herbs and making micro-salads with baby greens. With his knowledge and experience as a chef and then an instructor, he defined the taste and aroma of each herb as well as how to pair it with dishes that would complement each other. This cookbook is for students, food lovers, or those who love to cook. It will take you and your dinner guests on wonderful culinary adventures. You will also learn how to preserve and use these delicious herbs.

Happy discoveries!

*Daniel Baillard*
*Herbes Daniel*

# Introduction

After the long winter, when the sun melts the last snow banks, we are always happy to see the earth's colours again. We can't help but get excited, trying to imagine what our vegetable garden will look like by the end of the summer. We dream of its intoxicating scent.

The layout of the garden becomes the heart of family discussions every evening. Which herbs need sunlight, which ones prefer shade, and which ones need a lot of water? Then the real work begins: digging, raking, feeding the soil, and planting.

Each morning we check for the first buds. In a few weeks, a colourful mosaic will cover the earth. We rejoice when we can finally cut off a sprig of rosemary to season lamb chops for dinner. And then the basil will be used for pastas, cumin for sautés, and sorrel for sauces. Day by day, herbs will add zest to all our favourite dishes. The magic of herbs awakens our senses in spring and invites them to a summer-long party!

Until, one fine morning, the leaves on the trees begin to change colour. Before the first frost, be sure to harvest all the herbs still in the garden. To take full advantage of herbs throughout the winter, learn how to handle and preserve them.

# History

"The Lord hath created medicines out of the Earth, and he that is wise will not abhor them," recommended Ecclesiastes. But well before the Bible made allusions to using plants as medicine, phytotherapy—the medicinal use of natural plant extracts—had already been created, was widespread, and passed on through ancient civilizations.

It is remarkable that all civilizations, on all continents, developed and appropriated plant culture as food and researched its therapeutic qualities. A prime example of this is the extraction of opium from poppies 4,000 years before we learned how to extract morphine from opium. Great epochs in human history have discovered the culinary and medical benefits of wild plants as well as cultivated plants.

During the Egyptian, Greek, and Roman periods, a great deal of empirical knowledge was passed down, particularly through Arabic peoples, to their descendants. However, from the Renaissance and beyond, Western scholars emphasized a return to scientific thinking. As travel increased, and discoveries accumulated, more and more knowledge was acquired, necessitating a rigorous system for the classification of information.

At the beginning of the 16th century, a Swiss doctor, Paracelsus, tried to get to the heart or to the "quintessence" of plants, that is, where their therapeutic benefits came from. Since he did not have the tools of modern technology at his disposal, Paracelsus tried to relate the benefits of plants to their structural properties of form and colour. An Italian doctor and naturalist, Pietro Andrea Matthioli,

noted the work of a Greek physician, Pedanius Dioscorides, and discovered the properties of horse chestnut and European sarsaparilla.

At the end of the 17th century, via modern science, the knowledge of plants was extended and broadened to an extraordinary degree, in particular through specialized disciplines like paleontology—the scientific study of fossils—which led to other areas of discovery, including geography, cytology (the study of cells), genetics, histology (the study of tissues), and biochemistry.

Following on the work and efforts of numerous botanists throughout the centuries, it was a Swede, Carl Linnaeus, who classified plants in his famous tract, *Systema Naturae*, in 1735.

The use of microscopes in the middle of the 17th century allowed closer observation of the makeup of plants. These developments led to the definition of the cell—the fundamental building block of all animal or plant tissue—in the 19th century. This was the beginning of histology, or the science of tissues. These discoveries inevitably led scientists to begin substituting synthetic products for plant-based products.

But does this mean that plants have lost their mystery or their utility?

No, and for many reasons. To begin with, certain chemical components found in plants and used in medicine cannot be reproduced synthetically—yet. Just because the Japanese can make faux-crab, doesn't mean there will be synthetic salsify and celery.

*Basil*

*Lettuce Leaf Basil*

*Globe Basil*

*Purple Basil*

# BASIL

## *Ocimum basilicum (Linnaeus)*

### Lamiaceae Family

Originally from India, basil is now found all over the world. This rapidly growing species derives its name from the Greek *okimon*, meaning quick. Its fragrance gave it the royal qualifier, *basilikon*, making basil a favourite ornamental plant in gardens. It was a sacred plant for Hindus and it represented mourning for Greeks and love for the Romans.

The plant measures 40 cm at most and its oval leaves end in a pointed tip. It has white or purple-blue flowers grouped in clusters. The aroma of basil is intense, flowery, and fresh. It has a warm, spicy anise flavour with an herbaceous, slightly bitter aftertaste. The character of basil changes very slowly and the soft notes introduced by linalool, which are very pronounced in the beginning, fade beneath the anise flavour. Linalool (an essential oil) is a compound with a strong floral scent also found in abundance in coriander and Brazilian rosewood essences.

## Other Names

*Sweet basil Thai basil, Common basil, Saint Joseph's wort.*

## Cooking Uses

*When freshly picked, basil is very aromatic. It pairs nicely with fish, certain sauces and soups, and with pasta, of course, as well as being the basic ingredient of pesto. It goes extremely well with mustard.*

## Therapeutic Uses

*Antispasmodic, antiseptic, antidepressant, carminative, expectorant, heating agent, adrenal tonic, light sedative, antiemetic, galactagogue (see herb glossary for definitions).*

## Preservation

*At the end of summer, basil can be dried away from light at a temperature of less than 35°C. The taste of dried basil is quite bland.*

## Specifics

*The Egyptians used basil with myrrh, sage, and thyme to embalm the dead. In India, basil is placed on the chest of the dead to open the door to paradise. In Italy, it was carried by courtiers from the countryside as a symbol of love and fidelity.*

## Cucumber Cream with Basil Tomato Flakes

4 servings

*This is an excellent chilled soup for the summer that your guests will enjoy. Don't forget to prepare the basil tomato flakes the night before.*

- The night before, prepare the "flakes" by mixing the tomato juice and basil. Season it with salt and pepper. Pour into a shallow pan and put it in the freezer. The mixture will become flaked or slivered.
- The next day, sprinkle the cucumbers with coarse salt and stir. Let sit for 1 hour to draw out the excess water. Rinse, dry, and keep in the fridge.
- About 30 minutes before serving, quickly blend the cucumbers in a food processor. Add the cream, salt, and pepper.
- Serve immediately in very cold dishes and cover with the tomato basil flakes.

## INGREDIENTS

- 1 1/4 cups (300 ml) tomato juice
- 4 cups (100 g) basil, very finely chopped
- Sea salt and ground white pepper
- 3 cucumbers peeled, seeds removed, cut in half lengthwise and then into 1/2" (1 cm) pieces
- 3 teaspoons coarse salt
- 1 cup (250 ml) heavy cream (35%)

## INGREDIENTS

- 1 cup (250 ml) heavy cream (35%)
- 4 veal escalopes, 5 oz (150 g) each
- Salt and pepper
- Flour
- 1/4 cup (60 ml) peanut oil
- 1/2 cup (120 g) unsalted butter
- 1/2 cup (90 g) shallots, finely chopped
- 1/2 cup (125 ml) white wine
- 1/4 cup (60 ml) port wine
- 1 cup (250 ml) brown veal stock (p. 131) or store-bought demi-glace
- 1/2 cup (125 ml) cream
- 4 cups (100 g) basil, finely chopped

## Veal Escalopes with Basil Cream

4 servings

*Remember that the flavour of basil is short-lived. If you have a surplus of basil at the end of the summer, make pistou or pesto, which can be kept over the winter.*

- Reduce the cream by half.
- Flatten the veal escalopes with a mallet or rolling pin. Season both sides with salt, pepper, and flour.
- In a heavy-bottom pan, heat the oil and 1/4 cup (60 g) of butter. Cook the veal quickly on high heat and keep warm.
- Remove the cooking fat from the pan and heat the rest of the butter. Add the shallots, wine, and port. Reduce by half. Add the veal stock. Check the seasoning and set aside.
- Just before serving, add the cream, basil, and adjust the seasoning. Sauce the veal and serve immediately with pasta, rice, or potatoes.

### Pistou

- 6 cups (150 g) mashed basil leaves, 1 oz (30 g) finely chopped garlic, and a sufficient amount of olive oil.

### Pesto

- 6 cups (150 g) mashed basil, 1/3 cup (40 g) Parmesan, 1 oz (30 g) finely chopped garlic, and a sufficient amount of olive oil.

*Bay Leaf*

# BAY LEAF

## *Laurus nobilis* (*Linnaeus*)

### Lauraceae Family

Venerated by the Greeks and Romans, laurel (bay) was dedicated to Apollo. Its name is derived from the Latin *laudare*, meaning "to lease or rent." In Roman antiquity, it was braided into crowns to honour poets, victorious generals, and competition winners. Today, students obtain their baccalaureate (*baccae laurae* = bay berries) on completing their studies.

Laurel is an evergreen shrub with smooth bark that reaches 8 m high. It has dark green coriaceous (leather-like) leaves with characteristic rippled edges. The small yellow or white flowers bloom differently on the plant, depending on whether it is male or female.

## Other Names
*Sweet bay, bay tree, laurel, true laurel, Grecian laurel, noble laurel.*

## Cooking Uses
*Bay has a spiced, balsamic flavour. Its bitter, hot taste has acquired a well-deserved name. Indispensable in making bouquet garni and many other spice blends, it flavours steamed dishes, spiced soups, pickles, vegetables, mushrooms, brines, and vinegars.*

## Therapeutic Uses
*Antiseptic, sedative, stimulant. Oil extracted from the drupes is called laurel oil. It works wonders on painful joints.*

## Preservation
*Air dry it in temperatures less than 35$^0$C. Bay leaves keep very well out of light in an airtight container.*

## Specifics
*Do not mistake sweet bay, which is edible, with similar looking oleander or Portugal Laurel, which are very poisonous. Laurel was a symbol of victory for the Romans.*

## Bay Leaf Flavoured Roast Sturgeon

**4 servings**

*Your butcher can give you caul fat. It is the transparent, fatty membrane that surrounds pork or veal intestines. One of its many uses is to hold together chopped or minced ingredients during cooking. Sturgeon was a dish reserved for kings in the 16th and 17th centuries. Even though this high-quality fish is abundant in Canada, it is often overlooked. The flavour is somewhat neutral but, when judiciously used, a hint of bay can enhance the flavour. This dish should be enjoyed very hot.*

- In a food processor, mix the salmon, salt, and pepper. Add the egg white and mix for 20 seconds. Add the cream and adjust the seasoning.
- Butterfly the sturgeon and season with salt and pepper. Spread the stuffing evenly over the sturgeon and close. Wrap each piece of fish in caul fat and set aside in the fridge.
- In a bit of salted water, cook the onions until half-done. Drain and set aside. Do the same with the bacon and mushrooms.
- In a sauté pan, heat the butter and sear the fish to brown it on all sides. Sprinkle the onions, bacon, and mushrooms on top. Add the wine and bay leaves. Cook in the oven at 400°F (200°C) for 6 to 7 minutes, basting frequently. The internal temperature should read 155°F (68°C). Serve a piece of sturgeon in the centre of the plate with the garnish around it.

### Vegetables
- Roasted new potatoes, noisettes, or parisiennes

## INGREDIENTS

- 4 oz (120 g) fresh salmon
- Salt and pepper
- 1 egg white
- 1/3 cup (75 ml) heavy cream (35%), very cold
- 4 sturgeon fillets, 4 oz (120 g) each
- 4 small pieces of caul fat
- 12 small onions, peeled
- 3 slices of bacon, cut in thin matchsticks
- 5 oz (150 g) mushrooms, diced
- 1/4 cup (60 g) unsalted butter
- 1 cup (250 ml) white wine
- 3 g bay leaves, powdered

## INGREDIENTS

- 1 cup (250 ml) white wine
- 8 cups (2 L) light rabbit stock or store-bought chicken stock
- 2 bay leaves
- 1 bouquet garni without thyme
- 1 sprig of thyme
- 4 cups (1 L) milk
- Salt and pepper
- 2 lb (1 kg) cardoons, peeled and cut into sticks
- 1 whole rabbit, 2 1/2 lb (1.2 kg)
- 1/2 cup (125 ml) peanut oil
- Flour
- 7 oz (210 g) mirepoix (diced celery, carrots, onions)
- 2 cloves of garlic
- 13 oz (400 g) potatoes parisiennes

## Sautéed Rabbit with Cardoons Steamed with Bay

**4 servings**

*Cardoon is a garden vegetable, also known as artichoke thistle. The stalk between the leaves is eaten. In Quebec, it is easily found when in season.*

- In a pot, heat the wine and rabbit stock. Add the bay leaves, bouquet garni, and thyme, and simmer for 30 minutes. Set aside.
- Heat the milk, salt, and add the cardoons. Cook for 12 minutes. Keep cardoons in the cooking liquid.
- Cut the rabbit into equal pieces and season with salt and pepper. Heat the oil in a Dutch oven. Flour the pieces of rabbit and brown them to an even colour.
- Remove the excess cooking fat from the Dutch oven and pour in the bay stock. Add the mirepoix and garlic. Simmer slowly at 205°F (95°C) until three-quarters done, meaning the meat is not tender and a knife is difficult to remove when inserted.
- Add the drained cardoons and potatoes. Continue cooking slowly, and baste often. At this point, a knife should be easily removed from the meat. The vegetables should be "à pointe," or just done. Serve very hot.

*Chervil*

*Wild Chervil*

# CHERVIL

## *Anthriscus cerefolium (Linnaeus)*

### Apiaceae Family

Chervil was known to the people of antiquity and was widely cultivated in the Middle Ages, when its many benefits were recognized. The Romans also appreciated its usefulness.

Chervil is an annual plant and can reach a height of 70 centimetres. Its roots are fusiform (spindle-shaped) and tender. The soft leaves are fernlike and divided by minuscule small white flowers that form umbels. The hollow stem is covered in fine hairs. Different environments and the science of horticulture have promoted the growth of many varieties: flat-leaf, curly-leaf, and bulbous.

## Other Names
*Garden chervil, French parsley.*

## Cooking Uses
*This aromatic herb has a subtle delicateness and is used only fresh and uncooked. Heat volatizes (i.e., vaporizes or evaporates) the essential aroma. The fresh leaves, cut with scissors, give a pleasant fragrance to salads, cheeses, omelettes, scrambled eggs, and soups. Its spicy flavour goes well with rabbit, lamb, poultry, and delicate fish. Chervil is delicious in some sauces served both cold and hot.*

## Therapeutic Uses
*Bronchitis, liver, herpes, diuretic, eczema.*

## Preservation
*It is best to eat chervil fresh because of its delicate taste. Vacuum packing can preserve its aromatic flavours.*

## Specifics
*Chervil contains high levels of vitamin C, a bitter taste, and the same flavonoid glycoside that is found in parsley. It is also used in cleansing infusions. Its juice calms coughs when added to milk or warm tea.*

## Steamed Trout, Chervil Jus, and Creamed Cauliflower

4 servings

- Heat the milk and cream, and season with salt and pepper. Process the cauliflower florets in the food processor until they are seed size, and cook in the cream and milk until they are tender, but still *al dente*. Drain the cauliflower, reserving the cream.
- Butterfly the trout fillets.
- Heat the fish stock in the bottom of a steamer. Place the fillets in the basket of the steamer and season with salt and pepper. Bring stock to a boil and steam fish to an internal temperature of $160^0$F ($70^0$C).
- While the fish is steaming, put the olive oil, cayenne, and chervil in a blender and drizzle in the cauliflower cooking cream and milk to make the jus.
- Heat the cauliflower in a non-stick pan and add the hemp seeds. Press the cauliflower and hemp seed mixture into a stainless steel mould or a cookie cutter. Place a trout fillet on top of the cauliflower and hemp seed mixture and pour the chervil jus around it.

**INGREDIENTS**

- 1 cup (250 ml) milk
- 1 cup (250 ml) heavy cream (35%)
- 13 oz (400 g) cauliflower florets
- 4 trout fillets, 4 oz (120 g) each
- Salt and pepper
- 1 cup (250 ml) reduced fish stock
- 1/4 cup (60 ml) olive oil
- Cayenne
- 2 oz (60 g) chervil
- 1 1/3 oz (40 g) hemp seeds, toasted

## INGREDIENTS

- 1/2 cup (120 g) butter
- 1 onion, minced
- 1 leek, minced
- 3 cups (100 g) sorrel leaves
- 3 cups (100 g) nettle leaves
- 1/2 cup (100 g) celery, diced
- 3 cups (100 g) purslane leaves
- 2 cups (60 g) parsley, stems removed
- 2 cups (500 ml) chicken broth
- Salt and pepper
- 8 oz (240 g) potato, diced
- Small country bread croutons
- 1 cup (30 g) chervil leaves

## Madame St. Pierre's End-of-Season Herb Broth
4 servings

*At the end of summer, when the first frost touches the last vegetables and herbs in the garden, Madame St. Pierre, chef emeritus from Rimouski, picks all the herbs, chops, and mixes them in a crock with coarse salt to preserve them over the winter as "herbes salées" (salt-preserved herbs).*

- Heat the butter in a small stock pot. Sweat the onions and leeks. Add the sorrel, nettles, celery, purslane, and parsley root. Let simmer for a few minutes. Pour in the chicken broth and season with salt and pepper. Simmer covered for about 10 minutes. Add the potatoes and cook for 10 minutes more.
- Mix everything in the blender. Adjust the seasoning and serve in very hot bowls on top of the country bread croutons. Garnish with the chervil.

*Chives in bloom*

*Chinese chives*

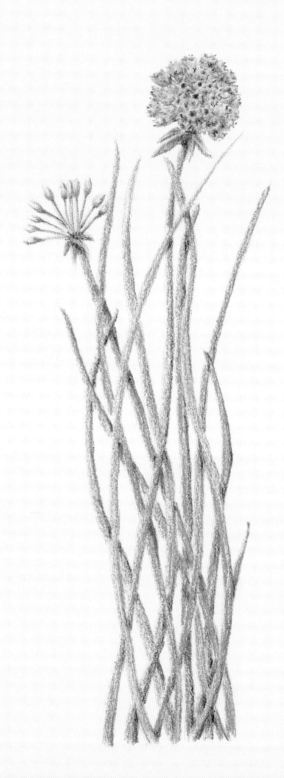

# CHIVES

*Allium schoenoprasum (Linnaeus)*

Amaryllidaceae Family

Chives were known in the Middle Ages as "rush leeks," from the Greek *schoinos*, signifying "rush," and *prason*, "leek." The famous botanist Carl Linnaeus, who was partial to poached eggs sprinkled with chives, gave the plant its Latin name. Today it grows all over the world.

Chives stem from small bulbs and grow in clusters. The pink or purplish flowers grow just above the green stems. The flavour of chives resembles onions, but with more delicate, less intense, nuances.

## Cooking Uses

*This little bulb grows in tufts and yields small stalks that flavour omelettes, salads, and green sauces marvellously. Minced chives mixed with chervil or parsley can enhance many dishes.*

## Therapeutic Uses

*Demulcent, antiscorbutic, antiseptic, antitussive, cardiotonic, cicatrizant, diuretic, emollient, expectorant, hypoglycemant, laxative (see herb glossary for definitions)*

## Preservation

*Chives don't stand up well to drying. However, they can be stored in the fridge for a few months or, even better, in the freezer.*

## Specifics

*Chives have the ability to lower blood pressure and to ease rheumatic pain. Chives are rich in vitamin C and contain carotene, vitamins A and B, sodium, calcium, potassium, phosphorous, and iron. They also contain an essential oil stocked with sulphur compounds.*

## INGREDIENTS

- 4 slices of calf's liver, 4 to 5 oz (120 to 150 g) each
- 2/3 cup (150 g) unsalted butter
- Salt and pepper
- Flour
- 1 cup (250 ml) raspberry vinegar
- 1/2 cup (125 ml) unthickened brown veal stock (p. 131) or store-bought demi-glace
- 1 cup (60 g) chives, very thinly sliced

## Sautéed Calf's Liver with Chive Raspberry Jus

4 servings

*It is important to slice the calf's liver uniformly and to the same thickness. Calf's liver is exquisite when it is neither too thick nor too thin. Too thick and it takes on a soft, unpleasant consistency. Too thin and it toughens because it cooks too fast. Cooking until just done is ideal.*

- Choose a heavy-bottom pan large enough to sear the liver, and heat 1/4 cup (60 g) butter. Season the slices of liver with salt, pepper, and flour both sides. Sear the liver quickly for 30 seconds on each side and remove immediately from the pan.
- Remove the excess cooking fat from the pan and pour in the raspberry vinegar. Reduce by 95% to remove the acidity. Add the veal stock and chives. Finish the sauce with the rest of the butter. Adjust the seasoning and pour over the slices of liver.

### Vegetables

- Mashed potatoes
- Green beans

## Vegetable and Chive Sauté

4 servings

*Peel all the vegetables and ensure that the turnips and zucchini are the same size. All the vegetables should be cooked separately. The chicken broth will take on the flavour of the vegetables and can be served as a vegetable-flavoured chicken consommé.*

- Bring the chicken broth to a boil, season, and cook the beans. When they are sufficiently cooked, remove the beans and spread them on a shallow baking pan, making sure they are separated so they cool as quickly as possible. Repeat these steps with the snap peas and zucchini.
- Place the beans in the basket of a steamer or a steamer insert. Cover and steam to your liking. Steam each vegetable separately to a desired doneness. When all the vegetables are cooked, mix them together and set aside. A few minutes before serving, heat the butter in a large pan and sauté the vegetables until they brown slightly. Season with salt, pepper, and add the chives. Serve very hot.

## INGREDIENTS

- 4 cups (1 L) chicken broth
- 1 cup (200 g) green beans
- 3/4 cup (150 g) snap peas
- 1/2 cup (100 g) zucchini
- 3/4 cup (150 g) baby carrots
- 3/4 cup (150 g) small turnips
- 1 cauliflower
- 2/3 cup (150 g) butter
- Salt and pepper
- 1 cup (60 g) chives, cut finely

## INGREDIENTS

- 2 slices of white bread
- 2 slices of French gingerbread
- 1/2 cup (30 g) chives, very finely chopped
- 2 egg yolks
- 3 tablespoons milk
- 4 whitefish fillets, 4 to 5 oz (120 to 150 g) each
- Salt and pepper
- Flour
- 1 cup (240 g) butter
- Lemon quarters

## Spice Crusted Whitefish Fillets with Chives

**4 servings**

*Lake herring is a high-quality fish. It is called whitefish in Quebec and is from the same family as salmon and trout. In France, it is called "fera" or "lavaret." It is always preferable to leave the skin on the fish, but be sure to remove all the scales. Dry the fillets to remove as much excess moisture as possible.*

- In a food processor, pulse the slices of bread and gingerbread into fine, fresh (not dry) breadcrumbs. Place them in a bowl and add the chives.
- Whisk the egg yolks with the milk. Season the whitefish fillets on both sides with salt and pepper and flour. Dip them into the egg and milk mixture and then coat with the breadcrumbs.
- Gently heat butter in a cast-iron pan and add the fillets.
- The butter will be absorbed by the bread crumbs and will form a crust that will keep the fish moist. Cook for 5 minutes on each side. Serve the fillets immediately with lemon slices.

Vegetables
- Boiled potatoes or rice
- Carrots

*Coriander leaves*

*Coriander seeds*

# CORIANDER

## *Coriandrum sativum* (*Linnaeus*)

### Apiaceae Family

Coriander was cited in the Old Testament and has been used since the time of the pharaohs. People in antiquity acknowledged its aromatic and therapeutic qualities. In Rome, it was considered indispensable to cooking.

An herbaceous plant from the Middle East, coriander can measure 20 to 80 centimetres. Its rose-hued flowers in double umbels yield a uniquely characteristic fruit, spherical and ribbed. The fresh plant releases an intense odour that becomes more pleasant when dried. The ripe whole fruit when dried and ground is used as a condiment. It gives a pleasant fruity, spicy, sweetish flavour to cold Greek appetizers. Fresh coriander leaves are very popular in Asian cuisine.

## Other Names

*Arab parsley, Chinese parsley, cilantro.*

## Cooking Uses

*Coriander is used as a condiment in salads (leaves), in soups (leaves), and appetizers (seeds). It is also used to flavour beer, and can be mixed with salt and pepper to preserve meat.*

## Therapeutic Uses

*Internal uses: carminative, antispasmodic, migraine, cardiac arrhythmia, sedative, antiemetic, mild adrenal tonic, intestinal atony, expectorant. In the past, it was considered an aphrodisiac and helped memory (see herb glossary for definitions).*

## Preservation

*The fruit, about the size of a peppercorn, becomes pleasant tasting when dried. The dried leaves, however, lose their flavour.*

## Specifics

*The name coriander comes from the Greek* koris *(irritating) and* andros, *(man), alluding to the disagreeable smell of the fresh seeds. In books on magic charms from the Middle Ages, coriander was used in sachets to attract love. It was said also that pregnant women who ate coriander would have a resourceful or creative child.*

## INGREDIENTS

- 1 veal foot
- 1 onion
- 1 carrot
- 1 celery stalk
- 1 bouquet garni
- 1/2 a bay leaf
- 2 cloves
- Oil for frying
- 1 Mexican chili, finely chopped
- 2 garlic cloves, finely chopped
- 2 cans of Stimpson's surf clams (keep the juice) or 5 oz (150 g) thawed clams
- 1 cinnamon stick
- 1 piece of star anise
- 1 piece of dried orange peel
- 1 piece of licorice
- Salt and pepper
- 1 1/3 cups (60 g) coriander leaves

# Coriander Stimpson's Surf Clams and Veal Foot
4 servings

*This smooth, triangular shellfish is very common in Quebec and deserves to be better known as an ingredient in cooking. It can be eaten raw or cooked and replaced with scallops or other shellfish.*

- To make the broth, put the veal foot into a stock pot, cover with water, boil, and skim. Add the onion, carrot, celery, bouquet garni, bay leaf, and the cloves. Cook slowly for 1 to 1 1/2 hours, until the meat is fork tender. Drain the cooked veal foot and dry well. Strain the stock with a fine-mesh strainer and set aside.
- Dice the meat from the veal foot into 1/2" (1 cm) pieces and dry well. Heat the oil and fry the veal meat until golden. Drain on paper towels.
- Pour 1 tablespoon of the frying oil into a Dutch oven and sauté the chilies and garlic. Add the pieces of veal, the Stimpson clam juice, and finish by covering with the veal-foot cooking stock. Add the cinnamon, star anise, orange peel, and licorice. Simmer for 20 minutes and place the thinly sliced Stimpson clams on top.
- Season with salt and pepper, and sprinkle with coriander leaves just before serving.

## Vegetables
- Steamed potatoes
- Parsnips

## Stuffed Chicken Thighs with Coriander

4 servings

*Ask your butcher to debone the chicken thighs without cutting them open. Fingerlings are yellow-fleshed potatoes that hold up well to cooking and do not turn black once cooked. Another advantage is they do not absorb water. They are readily available in most stores.*

- To make the stuffing, run all the ingredients twice through a meat grinder, using a medium disc. Mix well with the meat grinder's cutting disc.
- Mix the stuffing with the shallots, 1 1/3 cups (60 g) of the finely chopped coriander, egg, salt, and pepper.
- Season the inside and outside of the chicken thighs with salt and pepper. Stuff them equally and set aside.
- In the bottom part of a steamer, place the onions, carrots, celery, thyme, garlic, wine, and the rest of the coriander leaves. Add 6 cups (1.5 L) of water. Slowly cook covered for about 30 minutes so the flavours are well infused into the liquid. At the end of cooking, add salt and pepper.
- Half an hour before serving, place the potatoes in the broth. Place the steamer basket on the base and arrange the chicken thighs in it. Cover and cook for 30 to 40 minutes at 200°F (95°C).
- Pour the cooking broth into consommé bowls with the small toasted croutons and place the chicken thighs in soup plates. Serve with the vegetables and potatoes.

## INGREDIENTS

- 7 oz (210 g) chicken stuffing (recipe below)
- 1/4 cup (45 g) shallots, finely chopped
- 3 1/3 cups (150 g) fresh coriander leaves
- 1 egg
- Salt and pepper
- 4 chicken thighs, deboned
- 1 onion, finely minced
- 1 carrot, cut finely
- 1 celery stalk, finely minced
- 1/4 bay leaf
- 1 sprig of thyme
- 2 cloves of garlic, unpeeled
- 1 cup (250 ml) dry white wine
- 8 fingerling potatoes
- 1 oz (30 g) small croutons, toasted

### Chicken Stuffing

- 3 1/2 oz (100 g) chicken thighs
- 3 1/2 oz (100 g) chicken livers
- 3 1/2 oz (100 g) pork loin
- 1 egg
- 1/4 cup (60 ml) Cognac

*Dill*

*Fennel*

# DILL

## *Anethum graveolens (Linnaeus)*

### Apiaceae Family

A close relative of fennel, dill gets its name from the Greek word *anethon*, which means anise or dill. Note the physical resemblance to fennel and the way they grow. This umbelliferous plant originated in Asia and was introduced to Europe by Charlemagne. It was considered a symbol of vitality by the Romans. They believed that its essential oils reinforced positive thinking. It is also mentioned in the works of St. Matthew, who wrote in the first century that dill was taxed along with mint and cumin.

This annual plant grows to 1.2 metres high. The stem is glabrous and has alternate leaves. It has small, yellow flowers, grouped in flat umbels, and the seeds are lens-shaped, flat, and winged. The whole plant releases a characteristic strong, fresh, spicy fragrance. It has a pleasant, sweetish taste that is most delicate when the flowers are blossoming.

## Other Names
*Dill, wild fennel, bastard fennel, false anise, Russian parsley, Swedish parsley, Lao coriander.*

## Cooking Uses
*Dill is often used to flavour sauerkraut, marinades, and dill pickles. It is excellent in salads, with some fish, and shellfish.*

## Therapeutic Uses
*Carminative, antispasmodic, mild diuretic, cough expectorant, galactogogue, migraine, digestive, painful menstruation, colic in infants, asthma (see herb glossary for definitions).*

## Preservation
*Dill can be dried and should be kept in the dark, in an airtight container.*

## Specifics
*Dill is sometimes called "bastard fennel" or "wild fennel," which comes from the Middle Ages when it was used to ward off evil spirits. Greeks placed dill leaves on their eyelids to fall asleep quickly.*

## Dill and Flounder Roulades

**4 servings**

*There are five families of fluke found on the East coast of Canada. In decreasing order of quality they are: grey sole, American plaice, yellowtail flounder, winter flounder, and fourspot flounder. Sole is imported from Europe.*

- Put the dill stems in a pot with the wine and 1/3 cup (60 g) of shallots. Boil for 30 minutes.
- Pour this liquid through a fine sieve and reduce it by 90%. Set aside.
- Flatten the flounder fillets (see technique p. 134). Season them with salt and pepper. Wrap the fillets around the chopped dill leaves and make the roulades. Arrange the fillets in a baking dish and surround them with the remaining shallots. Pour the dill essence over the dish and cover with a piece of greased parchment paper.
- Bake at 350°F (180°C) until small white dots appear on the surface of the fillets. Dry the fillets with paper towels and keep them warm. Pour the cooking liquid into a pot and add the cream. Thicken to your desired consistency with a slurry of potato starch thinned with water. Finish with the butter.
- Adjust the seasoning. Serve the roulades on individual plates with the sauce.

### Vegetables
- Steamed potatoes
- Rice
- Fennel bulbs
- Parsnips

## INGREDIENTS

- 2 bunches dill (stems roughly chopped, leaves finely chopped and kept separate from stems)
- 1 1/4 cups (300 ml) white wine
- 3/4 cup (135 g) shallots, finely chopped
- 12 flounder fillets
- Salt and pepper
- 1/4 cup (160 ml) heavy cream (35%)
- Potato starch
- 1/3 cup (80 g) unsalted butter

## INGREDIENTS

### Breadcrumbs

- 3 oz (90 g) dill seed
- 4 slices of white bread
- 2 cloves of garlic

- 8 lamb chops, bone in, 3 to 4 oz (90 to 120 g) each
- 1 oz (30 g) dill leaves, chopped
- 1/4 cup (60 ml) olive oil
- 1/2 teaspoon (2 g) thyme, powdered
- 1/2 teaspoon (2 g) bay leaves, powdered
- Salt and pepper
- 1/2 cup (125 ml) Dijon mustard
- 2/3 cup (150 g) unsalted butter

## Dill Crusted Lamb Chops

**4 servings**

*The meat should marinate for 12 to 24 hours. "Internal temperature" refers to the degree of doneness at the centre of a piece of meat.*

- To make the breadcrumbs, grind the dill seeds in a coffee grinder or spice grinder. In a food processor, process the slices of bread with the garlic cloves. Add the ground dill. Set aside.
- The night before the meal, marinate the lamb chops with the dill leaves, oil, thyme, and bay leaves. Season with salt and pepper. Cover with plastic wrap and keep in the fridge.
- Two hours before the meal, dry the lamb chops off well. In a heavy-bottom pan, heat the oil from the marinade and sear the chops on both sides so they are nice and brown but still "blue" inside. Cool. Brush the chops with mustard and coat them with the dill breadcrumbs.
- On the stove in a shallow baking pan, heat the butter. Add the lamb chops. Bake in the oven at 350°F (180°C) for about 30 minutes, turn them once during cooking. A crust will form around them. They are done when the internal temperature is 136°F (58°C). Lightly season the chops with salt and pepper. Serve immediately so the crust remains crunchy.

### Vegetables

- Green beans
- Carrot sticks
- Potatoes boulangères

*Hyssop*

# HYSSOP

## *Hyssopus officinalis*

### Lamiaceae Family

Hyssop, often cited in the Bible as a sacred plant, gets its name from Hebrew. It was called *Ezôb*. It was also very well known to the Arabic people. The Greeks made a brew with hyssop, lavender, and honey.

As with lavender and thyme, hyssop is a plant familiar to arid areas. Its long tufts do not grow past 50 centimetres and have small, straight, opposing leaves that often emerge from cracks in rocks and old walls. The blue or rose flowers are grouped in the axis of the leaves.

## Other Names
*Holy herb.*

## Cooking Uses
*The leaves are more perfumed than the flowers. However, the latter goes well in salads, particularly those made with maché (salad greens) and bee balm pistils.*

## Therapeutic Uses
*Promotes and alters expectoration, by attacking bronchial secretion stasis (the concentrate is excreted through the lungs). Antiseptic, emollient, stimulant, hypertensor, diuretic (see herb glossary for definitions).*

## Preservation
*Hyssop stands up well to drying. Suspend it in a warm, dark, well-ventilated place. Once dried, keep it out of light in an airtight container.*

## Specifics
*Hyssop is an essential ingredient in the making of Chartreuse, the liqueur made by Carthusian monks. The homemade version of this recipe is on p. 51. "Purge me with hyssop and I will be clean," said King Solomon. He used this sacred plant with cedar wood to ward off leprosy.*

## Pork Chops with Hyssop
**4 servings**

*It is important not to overcook the pork. Our grandparents overcooked it because of tapeworm. We know now that tapeworm, when present, is killed at $184^0F$ ($84^0C$). However, pork farms now are the model of hygiene so that tapeworm, in fact, no longer exists in pork.*

- Season the chops with salt and pepper and cover with the hyssop leaves. In a large heavy-bottom pan, heat the fat and cook the chops on both sides, on high heat, until they reach an internal temperature of $160^0F$ ($70^0C$).
- Drain the cooking fat from the pan and flambé the chops with the Chartreuse. Remove them from the pan and keep warm. In the same pan, pour in the liquid from the drippings, adjust the seasoning, and finish with butter.
- Pour 1 tablespoon of the jus onto each plate and place the chops on top. Sprinkle with the hyssop flowers.

### Vegetables
- Sautéed potatoes
- Parsnips
- Green beans

## INGREDIENTS

- 4 pork chops, 5 1/3 oz (160 g) each, bone in
- Salt and pepper
- 2 oz (60 g) hyssop leaves, finely chopped
- 1/2 cup (120 g) fat from pork drippings
- 1/2 cup (125 ml) homemade Chartreuse-style liqueur (p. 51)
- 1 cup (250 ml) liquid from pork drippings
- Butter
- 2 oz (60 g) hyssop flowers

## INGREDIENTS

- 2 cups (500 ml) fromage blanc
- 3 rounds petit-suisses cheese
- 1/2 cup (90 g) shallots, finely chopped
- 2 oz (60 g) hyssop leaves, finely chopped
- Salt and pepper
- 1/3 cup (75 ml) heavy cream (35%)
- 2 tablespoons dry white wine
- 2 teaspoons sunflower oil
- 1/2 clove of garlic, minced
- 2/3 oz (20 g) hyssop flower pistils
- Toasted slices of bread

---

- 32 g (1 oz) fresh angelica
- 16 g (3 tsp) cinnamon
- 4 g (1 tsp) saffron
- 4 g (1 tsp) mace
- 1 L (4 cups) alcohol, 45%
- 1.2 kg (5 cups) fructose
- 100 g (3 1/2 oz.) fresh lemon balm
- 100 g (3 1/2 oz) fresh hyssop

## Hyssop-Flavoured Fromage Blanc
4 servings

*In the region of Lyon, France, there is a well-known recipe for fresh fromage blanc, called Cervelle de Canut and also known as Claqueret, which is an herbed cream cheese. Excellent fromage blanc is also made in Quebec and is just as delicious. Hyssop can be found in large supermarkets in season.*

- Mix all the ingredients well, except the hyssop flower pistils and the bread. Pour into a ramekin and keep in the fridge.
- Turn the ramekin over onto a plate to remove the cheese and sprinkle with the hyssop pistils. Serve with the toasted slices of bread.

## Homemade Chartreuse-Style Liqueur
4 servings

*This enticing recipe comes from phytotherapist, aromatherapist, and talented author, Doctor Jean Valnet. The liqueur can be used to deglaze beef tournedos, veal escalope, chicken breasts, etc.*

- Macerate all the ingredients, except the lemon balm and hyssop, and keep in a closed container out of light for at least a dozen days.
- Mince the hyssop and lemon balm and put into a coffee filter. Pour the macerating alcohol over it. Bottle it and store.

*Common lavender*

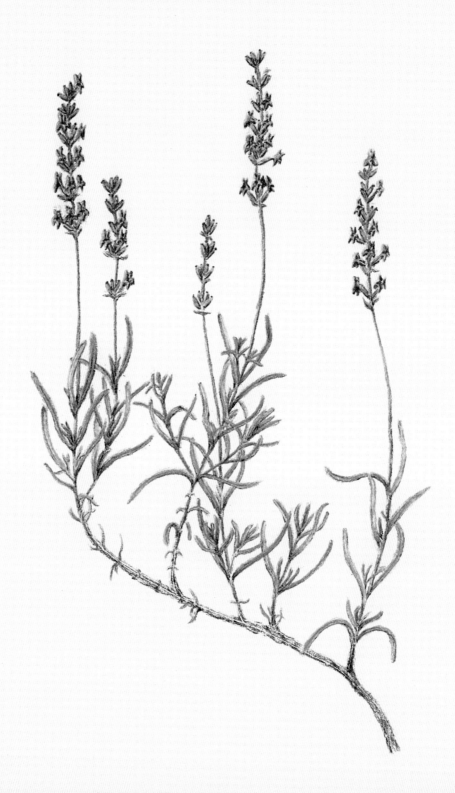

# LAVENDER

## *Lavandula officinalis (Chaix)*

### Lamiaceae Family

Lavender comes from the Mediterranean. The Romans used it to relax by infusing their baths with it. The name comes from *lavare*, which means to wash. Lavender is cultivated mainly for the fragrance of its essential oil. It is used in perfumes and by herbalists for its therapeutic benefits.

Lavender grows in tufts. It is easily recognized by its thin, square-shaped stems, its whitish, linear leaves, and little blue flowers in vertical spikes.

## Other Names
*Lavendula, English lavender, French lavender, garden lavender.*

## Cooking Uses
*In small quantities, lavender has the power to elevate mediocre dishes and make them more appetizing. Recently, lavender has moved up in the culinary arts, especially in the world of pastries.*

## Therapeutic Uses
*Antispasmodic, antiseptic, cholagogue, diuretic, cardiac tonic, antirheumatic, emmenagogue, hypertensor, antivenin, cicatrizant (see herb glossary for definitions).*

## Preservation
*Dry the leaves, flowers, and pistils out of light and keep in an amber airtight container at a cool temperature.*

## Specifics
*The antiseptic and antivenin properties of lavender are highly valued. The plant can be life-saving simply by rubbing the flowers over a bite from a poisonous animal or insect.*

# Lavender Arctic Char Papillotes

**4 servings**

*The two main ingredients in this recipe are very delicate, so handle them carefully! The lavender used here should have very small leaves and can be found in speciality stores. You will be intoxicated by the exquisite fragrance when you open the papillotes—a delightful prelude to enjoyable eating.*

- Season the fish with salt and pepper on both sides. Cut squares of aluminum foil, about 2 to 3 inches (5 to 7.5 cm) larger than the fish fillets. Use a brush to generously oil the foil squares and spread half of the lavender on the foil. Place the fish on top and cover with the rest of the lavender and the shallots. Close the papillotes, leaving a small hole open at the top to pour in the wine. Close tightly.
- In a shallow baking pan filled with half a glass of water, bake the papillotes in the oven at 400⁰F (200⁰C) for about 15 minutes. The papillotes will inflate during cooking.

## Vegetables
- Steamed potatoes

## INGREDIENTS

- 4 arctic char fillets, 6 oz (180 g) each
- Salt and pepper
- 1/2 cup (120 g) unsalted butter
- 7 oz (210 g) fresh lavender leaves
- 1/2 cup (90 g) dried shallots, finely chopped
- 1 cup (250 ml) dry white wine

## INGREDIENTS

- 1/2 cup (125 ml) peanut oil
- 1/4 cup (60 g) unsalted butter
- 2 veal shanks, bone in
- 12 endives
- 12 cipollini onions or pearl onions
- 1 1/4 cups (300 ml) dry white wine
- 1 1/4 cups (300 ml) light veal stock (p. 130) or store-bought chicken broth
- Salt and pepper
- 1/2 a bay leaf
- 2 oz (210 g) lavender leaves, very finely chopped

## Veal Shank with Endives and Lavender

4 servings

*The veal shanks will release a lot of collagen while they cook, which is absorbed by the lavender and the endive. Choose a heavy-bottom pot, preferably cast iron, large enough to hold the shanks and endives.*

- Heat the oil and butter in a pot and brown the shanks evenly. At the same time, remove the bitter hearts from the endives (see p. 135) and peel the onions.
- Remove the excess cooking fat from the pan and deglaze with the wine. Arrange the endives and onions side by side. Pour in the veal stock. Add the salt, pepper, and bay leaves. Cover and cook in the oven at 400°F (200°C) for 1 to 2 hours (depending on the size of the shanks), until the shanks and endives are fork tender. Baste often. If liquid evaporates during cooking, it is important to add more.
- Remove the shanks, endives, and onions from the pot. Add the lavender to the cooking liquid. Simmer for 1 to 2 minutes and pour over the shanks.

*Lemon balm*

# LEMON BALM

## Melissa officinalis (Linnaeus)

### Lamiaceae Family

Writers from antiquity mentioned lemon balm but were not much interested in it. In the 10th century, however, Arabic people praised its power as a cordial and as a remedy for melancholia. This theory was revived by an herbalist at the beginning of the 20th century, who claimed that lemon balm had the power to dispel fits of bad temper in young people.

An evergreen plant of 20 to 80 centimetres, it has branching, straight stalks from the base, large, oval petioles, dentate leaves with prominent ribs. The flowers are yellowish, then white or rose.

## Other Names
*Citronella, sweet balm, honey plant.*

## Cooking Uses
*Its name in French—mélisse—derives from the Greek word meaning "honey bee." When young, lemon balm releases a pleasant lemon fragrance. It can be used in mixed salads or with fish and lean meats.*

## Therapeutic Uses
*Stimulating effects on the brain, heart, uterus and the digestive system. Antispasmodic, physical and intellectual stimulant, stomachic, carminative, vermifuge (see herb glossary for definitions).*

## Preservation
*Lemon balm leaves can be dried but the aroma does not last long.*

## Specifics
*Lemon balm is an ingredient in Chartreuse, Bénédictine, and eau de mélisse (Melissa Water, a herbal remedy made up of 14 herbs and spices). In the 17th century, it was used to fight depression. It was also recommended for digestive difficulties and palpitations.*

## INGREDIENTS

- 16 to 20 cups (4 to 5 L) court-bouillon (p. 131)
- 4 lobsters, 1 1/4 lbs (600 g) each
- 2 cans of lobster bisque or 1 2/3 cups (400 ml) lobster sauce (recipe below)
- 2/3 cup (150 g) butter
- 2 dried shallots, finely chopped
- 1/2 cup (125 ml) Cognac
- 2/3 cup (150 ml) white wine
- 1 cup (250 ml) heavy cream (35%), reduced by 50%
- 2 oz (60 g) lemon balm leaves, finely chopped
- Salt and pepper

## Lobster Sauce

- 2 lb (900 g) lobsters, or lobster shells
- 1/4 cup (60 ml) olive oil
- 3 tablespoons unsalted butter
- 2 tablespoons shallots, chopped
- 1/2 clove of garlic, sprout removed, chopped
- 1/2 cup (125 ml) cognac
- 1/2 cup (125 ml) white wine
- 3 1/2 cups (875 ml) reduced fish stock (fumet) (p. 131)
- 1 oz (30 g) tomato paste
- 1 tsp (5 g) parsley, roughly cut
- ¼ tsp (1 g) cayenne
- 1 teaspoon salt

# Madeleine Island Lobster Scented with Lemon Balm
4 servings

- In a large pot, cook two lobsters at a time in the court-bouillon for 3 minutes. Cool the four lobsters in the court-bouillon, so they are infused with the aromatic herbs and vegetables.
- Shell the lobsters and remove the meat. Cut the tails in half and leave the claw meat whole.
- Heat the lobster bisque. At the same time, in a sauté pan, heat 1/3 cup (80 g) of butter and slowly sauté the shallots. Add the lobster and flambé with the Cognac. Pour in the wine and reduce by 90% to remove the acidity.
- Add the reduced cream and pour in the lobster bisque. Simmer slowly and finish the sauce with the rest of the butter. Add the lemon balm just before serving. Season with salt and pepper to taste. Serve in soup bowls with boiled potatoes.

## Lobster Sauce (8 servings)

- Cut the lobster tails into steaks and break the claws. Cut the body in two, lengthwise. Remove the gravel pouch, found close to the head. Set aside the creamy yellow parts and the meat.
- In a sauté pan, heat the oil and butter. Sear the shell pieces to a deep red colour. Remove excess fat and add the other ingredients.
- Cover and cook at 400 to 450$^0$F (200 to 230$^0$C) for about 30 minutes. Drain the pieces of shell and crush them in a fine sieve with a pestle to extract the maximum amount of liquid from the shells. Put the extracted liquid in the sauce with the creamy parts of the lobster and the lobster meat. Reduce, cooking on high heat while whisking. Strain through a fine sieve lined with cheese cloth. Keep in the fridge until used.

## Sautéed Chicken Supremes with Lemon Balm Sauce

4 servings

- Bring the chicken stock to a boil. Add the lemon balm, lemon juice, and garlic. Simmer for 15 minutes, cover, and let it infuse.
- Season the chicken breasts with salt and pepper. Heat the butter in a sauté pan and gently brown the chicken to a nice even golden colour. Remove the cooking oil from the pan and deglaze with the white wine. Reduce by 95% and add the lemon balm broth. Cook slowly to obtain an internal temperature of $170^0$F ($75^0$C).
- Remove the chicken from the pan and thicken the sauce with the white roux. Strain the sauce through a fine sieve, adjust the seasoning, and serve nice and hot.

## INGREDIENTS

- 1 1/4 cups (300 ml) light chicken stock (p. 130)
- 3 1/3 oz (100 g) lemon balm leaves, chopped
- Juice of one lemon
- 1 clove of garlic, whole
- Salt and pepper
- 4 chicken breasts, 5 to 6 oz (150 to 180 g) each
- 4 oz (120 g) unsalted butter
- 1 cup (250 ml) dry white wine
- White roux (p. 132)

*Marjoram*

*Oregano*

# MARJORAM

## *Origanum majorana* (*Linnaeus*)

### Lamiaceae Family

Prized in antiquity, marjoram was used to make love potions. A Greek legend told of how Amarakos, a companion of the king of Cyprus, died of shame after inadvertently spilling a precious salve, and was transformed into the marjoram plant by the goddess Aphrodite. Marjoram was sacred to the Indian gods Shiva and Vishnu and, in Egypt, to the god Osiris.

It is a perennial plant 20 to 50 centimetres tall, with pale green, oval leaves and small white or rose flowers. The whole plant is covered in a greyish down and releases a pleasant scent.

## Other Names
*Sweet marjoram, wild marjoram, oregano.*

## Cooking Uses
*Used in sauces, it enhances the flavour of meat. It can be used as a condiment in marinades, to create spice blends for stuffing, stews, and sauces, and especially in tomato sauce. It goes well with salads, fish, and vegetables. In recipes, oregano can be used as a substitute.*

## Therapeutic Uses
*Strong bactericidal, antispasmodic, hypotensor, vasodilator, carminative, expectorant, digestive (see herb glossary for definitions). Recommended for insomnia.*

## Preservation
*Marjoram can be dried, out of light, in temperatures less than 35°C.*

## Specifics
*Marjoram imparts flavour to beers and vermouths. It is also used in making perfumes and soaps. Do not confuse marjoram with oregano. In Quebec, the latter is used much more often than the former.*

## INGREDIENTS

### Stuffing

- 2 oz (60 g) duck thighs, trimmed
- 2 oz (60 g) duck liver
- 2 slices of bread
- 1/4 cup (60 ml) heavy cream (35%)
- 1 egg white
- 1 tablespoon potato starch or corn starch
- 1 1/4 cups (90 g) marjoram, chopped finely
- Salt and pepper

- 4 duck breasts, 8 oz (240 g) each
- Salt and pepper
- 2 oz (60 g) duck fat
- 2 oz (60 g) Armagnac
- 1/2 cup (125 ml) thickened brown duck stock (p. 130) or store-bought demi-glace
- 1/2 cup (120 g) butter

## Stuffed Duck Breast with Marjoram Jus

**4 servings**

*If the stuffing isn't cooked before filling the duck breasts, this dish will require more cooking time, which will overcook the duck and toughen the meat.*

- Grind the first six ingredients for the stuffing twice with a medium disc in a meat grinder. Add the marjoram, salt, and pepper, and mix well. Make 4 small rolls the same length as the duck breasts, wrap them in plastic wrap and tie the ends. Cook them in 212°F (100°C) water, for 5 to 6 minutes. Cool in cold water. Set aside.
- Butterfly the duck breasts and season with salt and pepper. Fill with the cooked rolls of stuffing. Close and season with salt and pepper. Set aside. In a sauté pan, heat the duck fat and sear the breasts skin side down for 2 to 3 minutes. Do the same for the other side. Put a lid on slightly askew and cook on medium heat for 7 to 8 minutes. Remove the excess cooking fat from the pan and flambé the breasts in Armagnac. Remove them from the pan and keep warm. In the same pan, add the thickened duck stock and finish the sauce with butter. Adjust the seasoning.
- Pour the sauce onto the bottom of the plate. Slice the breasts and serve on top of the sauce.

### Vegetables

- Crosnes (Chinese artichoke)
- Fingerling potatoes
- Green beans
- Spinach

## Fingerling Potato Confit with Marjoram

4 servings

- In a heavy-bottom pan, heat 2 oz (60 g) of duck fat and sauté the potatoes for 2 to 3 minutes. Put them in a baking dish and cover with the rest of the duck fat, the clove of garlic, and marjoram. Salt, pepper, and cook in the oven for 40 to 45 minutes at 350$^0$F (180$^0$C) or until fork tender.

## Sautéed Beef Prime Rib with Marjoram Jus

4 servings

- Season both sides of the prime ribs with salt and pepper and rub each of the 4 sides with 1/4 cup (10 g) of marjoram. Heat the oil and 1/4 cup (60 g) of the butter in a heavy-bottom broiling pan. Sear the ribs on each side to a nice even colour.
- Put the ribs in a 450$^0$F (230$^0$C) oven and baste occasionally. At 130$^0$F (54$^0$C), they will be rare, at 136$^0$F (58$^0$C), they will be medium. Always let the meat rest, keeping it warm, for 7 to 8 minutes before serving. While the beef is resting, make the jus. Remove the cooking fat from the broiling pan and deglaze with the wine and beef stock. Finish with the rest of the butter and adjust the seasoning.
- Pour a bit of the beef jus on the bottom of each plate. Slice the beef and place it in the jus.

### Vegetables
- Gratin dauphinois (potato gratin)
- French cut green beans

## INGREDIENTS

- 8 oz (240 g) duck fat
- 2 lb (1 kg) fingerling potatoes, peeled and dried off
- 1 clove of garlic
- 1/2 cup (20 g) marjoram leaves
- Salt and pepper

---

- Salt and pepper
- 2 beef prime ribs, 20 oz (600 g) each, bone in
- 1 cup (40 g) marjoram, finely chopped
- 1/3 cup (75 ml) peanut oil
- 1/2 cup (120 g) unsalted butter
- 1 cup (250 ml) dry white wine
- 3/4 cup (175 ml) light beef stock

*Wild mint*

*Peppermint*

*Garden mint*

*Pennyroyal*

# MINT

**Peppermint - *Mentha piperita* (*Linnaeus*) | Spearmint - *Mentha spicata* (*Linnaeus*)**

Lamiaceae Family

In Greek mythology, the nymph Mintha, Hades's lover, drew the wrath of Persephone, the wife of the god of the underworld. She took her revenge by transforming Mintha into mint, but she did not have the power to stop her from releasing an irresistible scent. Hippocrates and Aristotle believed mint was an aphrodisiac.

Spearmint: a perennial plant that can reach 1 metre in height. It has sessile, lanceolate, dentate leaves that are bright green. It releases a penetrating menthol scent with spicy and herbaceous notes. It has a pleasant aromatic flavour, with a light astringency and a hint of bitterness.

Peppermint: a non-fruiting hybrid that comes from crossbreeding three varieties of mint, all native to southern Europe.

## Cooking Uses

*Mint is used as an herbal tea for digestion after a meal and also in soups. Mint is a good accompaniment for lamb and mutton in many English dishes. Many desserts and sorbets use it as an accent. It is also used with cheeses, in cocktails, and in fresh fruit juices.*

## Therapeutic Uses

*Cardiac stimulant, galactophobia, carminative, antioxidant, antiviral, antifungal, nervous system stimulant, general tonic, emmenagogue, expectorant, vermifuge, antispasmodic (gastric, colic), general antiseptic (see herbal guide for definitions).*

## Preservation

*Harvested leaves will keep their aroma if dried in a dark place at a temperature less than 35°C.*

## Specifics

*Mint is used to make Bénédictine. In Arabic countries, delicious mint tea is sign of hospitality.*

## Varieties of Mint

*There are more than 600 known varieties of mint. Among these are peppermint, curly mint, apple mint, chocolate mint, water mint, lemon mint, field mint, pennyroyal mint, horse mint, wild mint, etc.*

## INGREDIENTS

- 4 pieces of bluefin tuna or another fish of your choice, 6 oz (180 g) each
- Salt and pepper
- 1/2 cup (90 g) shallots, finely chopped
- 6 springs of mint, minced (chop the leaves and stems separately and set aside)
- 1 cup (250 ml) dry white wine
- 6 tablespoons crème de menthe or peppermint extract
- 1/2 cup (125 ml) grape seed oil
- 3/4 cup (180 g) unsalted butter

## Atlantic Tuna with Mint Butter
### 4 servings

*Buy bluefin tuna the night before you use it. You can substitute big eye tuna, yellowfin tuna, albacore tuna, Atlantic bonito, and skipjack tuna.*

- Salt and pepper the tuna uniformly the night before. Put it in a container with an airtight lid. Place the shallots, mint stems (without the leaves), wine, crème de menthe, and half the oil around the fish. Cover with plastic wrap and the airtight lid and leave in the fridge for 24 to 36 hours, occasionally turning the pieces of tuna.
- Cover the butter with plastic wrap and leave at room temperature for at least 6 hours before the meal.
- Thirty minutes before cooking, drain and dry off the pieces of tuna. Reduce the marinade by 90% on high heat and Strain through a cone-shaped or fine mesh strainer. Press all the liquid out. Cool. Mix with the butter and set aside at room temperature. Add the reserved mint leaves into the reduced marinade and chill. Season it with salt and pepper. Pour into a gravy boat.
- Heat a grill pan or a cast-iron pan and brush the tuna with the rest of the oil. Sear the fish until the internal temperature is $145^0$F ($63^0$C), or less if you prefer it rare or blue.
- Rest the cooked tuna for 3 to 5 minutes. Serve with Chinese noodles. Place the mint butter on the tuna. It will melt onto the noodles and give the whole dish a beautiful aroma.

## Mint Liqueur

4 servings

- Infuse the mint leaves in alcohol for 2 months in a cupboard.
- Once this is completed, melt the sugar (fructose) into the water and cook until syrup is obtained. Skim and cool. Mix with the alcohol, preferably strained.
- To prepare the caramel, melt the sugar into the water and cook until it caramelizes to a golden colour. Stop the cooking. Add the caramel to the liqueur in small amounts to get the desired colour.

## Mint and Honey Braised Ham

4 to 6 servings

*Ask your butcher for a low-salt ham, which contains less salt than an ordinary ham. Put it in a pot and pour cold water over it, and leave for at least 1 to 2 hours.*

- In a large pot, boil the ham with the carrots, onions, celery, garlic, thyme, bay leaf, mint stalks, peppercorns, and cloves. Simmer gently at 205°F (95°C), until a skewer can be inserted into the ham and comes out easily. Leave the ham in the broth for at least 2 hours.
- Remove the ham from the broth and drain well. Remove the rind and some of the fat. Heat an oven-safe heavy-bottom pot and add the rind, fat, and the ham. Cover and cook in the oven at 400°F (200°C) for 30 minutes.
- Mix the honey and mint leaves together and brush the mixture on the ham. Pour in the wine and the pork stock and put back into the oven on broil until the ham turns light brown. Serve very hot with the jus.

### Vegetables
- Rice
- Carrots
- Snap peas

## INGREDIENTS

- 5 cups (200 g) mint leaves or verbena, preferably freshly picked, washed and dried
- 4 cups (1 L) alcohol, 45%
- 3 cups (720 g) fructose
- 1 cup (250 ml) water

### Caramel
- 1/4 cup (60 g) sugar
- 1/4 cup (60 g) water

---

- 3 1/3 lb (1.5 kg) raw cured ham, bone in
- 2 carrots, diced for mirepoix
- 1 onion, diced for mirepoix
- 1 celery stalk, diced for mirepoix
- 4 cloves of garlic, unpeeled
- 1 sprig of thyme
- 1/4 bay leaf
- 8 mint stalks, without leaves
- 20 peppercorns
- 2 cloves
- 1 cup (250 ml) mint honey
- 2 oz (60 g) mint leaves, finely chopped
- 1 1/4 cups (300 ml) white wine
- 1 1/4 cups (300 ml) pork stock (cooking liquid)

*Indian mustard*

# MUSTARD

Black Mustard - *Brassica nigra* (*Linnaeus*) | White Mustard - *Brassica alba* (Boissier)

Cruciferae Family

Four centuries ago, Theophrastus spoke of growing mustard, referring to the "mustard seeds" of the Gospels. Columella spoke of its use as a condiment or seasoning, by soaking the leaves in vinegar. Using a paste as a condiment, by grinding the seeds in verjuice (made from pressing sour, unripe grapes) or must (freshly pressed fruit juice that contains the skin and seeds), appeared during the 13th century. The word mustard appeared for the first time in 1288. It was derived from *mostarde*, meaning "burning or boiling must."

There are three types of mustard: black, white, and brown. It is an annual plant that can reach 1 to 2 metres in height. It has fruit or long siliques (seed pods) of 10 to 20 millimetres that hold seeds that are red, brown, yellow, or white, depending on the variety. The main kinds of mustard are Dijon, fruity and strong, mustard made with verjuice, and black mustard. The very spicy, extra-strong mustard is made with wine vinegar and black mustard.

## Other Names
*Wild mustard, black mustard.*

## Varieties of Mustard
*Dijon mustard, grainy mustard, powdered mustard, German mustard, English mustard, flavoured mustard (with herbs, horseradish, fruit, lemon, chilies, wine, liqueur, pepper, etc.).*

## Cooking Uses
*Mustard is the base for some sauces that go especially well with grilled meats and fish. It also enhances the taste of sandwiches and cold dishes. It goes well with other spices and herbs, reinforcing their flavour.*

## Therapeutic Uses
*Bronchitis, congestion, rheumatism, foot care, mucolytic, stimulant (see herb glossary for definitions).*

## Preservation
*Dried mustard seeds keep for a very long time.*

## Specifics
*Beginning in the 18th century, a mustard-based poultice was used to treat bronchitis.*

## INGREDIENTS

- 2 whole kidneys, 8 to 10 oz (240 to 300 g) each, with the surrounding fat
- Salt and pepper

### Sauce

- 1 cup (250 ml) dry white wine
- 1/2 cup (90 g) shallots, finely chopped
- 1/2 cup (125 ml) strong Dijon mustard
- 1/2 cup (125 ml) heavy cream (35%)
- 2/3 cup (150 ml) thickened brown veal stock (p. 131) or store-bought demi-glace
- 1/2 cup (20 g) chives, chopped

## Grilled Veal Kidneys with Mustard Sauce

4 servings

*It is important to choose high quality kidneys from milk-fed veal. Kidneys from a heavier butcher calf or grain-fed calf are too large and do not work for this recipe.*

- Cut the kidneys in two, lengthwise. Remove the urinary tract, as well as 80% of the fat that surrounds the kidneys. (Leave a little fat. It will moisten the kidneys during cooking.) Set aside in the fridge.
- To prepare the sauce, reduce the wine and the shallots by 90% in a pot on high heat. Add the mustard and whisk continuously for 1 to 2 minutes so it loses some of its acidity. Add the cream and the veal stock. Simmer for a few minutes. Adjust the seasoning and add the chives. Set aside.
- Heat a grill pan or griddle to hot. Season the kidneys with salt and pepper. Sear them until nicely browned. Lower the heat and continue to grill until they are cooked on the outside and a little pink in the centre. The longer kidneys are cooked, the tougher they become.
- Serve the kidneys on individual plates and top with the mustard sauce.

### Vegetables

- Mashed potatoes or rice pilaf
- Parsnips
- Broccoli
- Cauliflower

## Sautéed Chicken with Cassis Mustard

**4 servings**

*You can replace the cassis mustard with whatever mustard you like. You can also use Dijon mustard mixed with crème de cassis.*

- Dry the chicken thighs well and season with salt and pepper. Heat the oil in a sauté pan. Place the thighs flat in the pan and sear on all sides until they are nicely browned. Cook in the oven at $400^0$F ($200^0$C), basting regularly. When the internal temperature reaches $150^0$F ($65^0$C), remove the cooking oil from the pan. Toss in the shallots and deglaze with the wine.
- Remove the thighs from the pan and set aside in a drip or broiling pan. Add the chicken stock, salt, and pepper to the deglazed pan. Finish the sauce with butter and set aside. Brush the thighs with the mustard and put back in the still hot oven. While continuing to cook, the mustard will form a crust and the acidity will disappear. When the temperature reads $180^0$F ($81^0$C) in the back of the thigh, they are cooked perfectly.
- Pour the jus into the bottom of each plate and place the thighs on top. The mustard crust will preserve the tenderness of the chicken.

### Vegetables
- Mashed potatoes
- Green beans
- Carrots
- Parsnips

## INGREDIENTS

- 4 chicken thighs, 6 to 7 oz (180 to 210 g) each
- Salt and pepper
- 1/3 cup (75 ml) cooking oil
- 1/3 cup (60 g) shallots, finely chopped
- 1 cup (250 ml) white wine
- 1/2 cup (125 ml) chicken stock
- 1/3 cup (80 g) butter
- Cassis mustard

## INGREDIENTS

- 3 1/3 oz (100 g) *herbes salées*
- 1/2 cup (125 ml) mayonnaise, homemade or store bought
- 1/4 cup (60 ml) Dijon mustard
- Lemon juice
- 3 oz (90 g) hazelnuts, chopped and toasted
- Salt and pepper
- 13 oz (400 g) whelks, precooked or canned, minced in equal pieces

## Whelk Salad with Remoulade Sauce
4 servings

*In Quebec, whelks, a type of sea snail, are mistakenly called periwinkles.*

- Boil the *herbes salées* in water to remove some of the salt. Repeat this step, if needed. Drain and dry well.
- Whisk together the mayonnaise, mustard, lemon juice, and the hazelnuts. If necessary, season with salt and pepper. Add the whelks and the *herbes salées*. Adjust the seasoning and serve chilled.

*Greater nettle*

# NETTLE

## Greater Nettle - *Urtica dioica* (*Linnaeus*) | Lesser Nettle - *Urtica urens* (*Linnaeus*)

### Urticaceae Family

For millennia, humans have used nettles as food and medicine. Originating in Eurasia, nettles were ignored by the newer schools of European and American medicine, but local people have always used them. Nettle has long been used in the textile industry to make a natural fabric, much like its cousin, hemp, which also produces a quality fibre.

Nettle is a dioecious perennial of 50 centimetres to 1.5 metres. It has tall, simple stalks with opposite leaves, oval at the base and downy, with triangular teeth. The flowers are green (June to October) and they grow off clusters of branches: 4 sepals, 4 stamens, and 1 ovary, brush-like stigma, ovoid achene fruit, 1 seed, and underground rhizomes. The flavour is astringent and sour.

## Other Names
*Stinging nettle, common nettle, burning nettle, dog nettle.*

## Cooking Uses
*Nettle soup is a cooking classic. Nettles should be picked before the stalks harden. They can be used like spinach, but contain more iron. The leaves go well with potatoes, leeks, watercress, cabbage, and legumes. Nettles should not be eaten raw.*

## Therapeutic Uses
*Antiemetic, antidiabetic, astringent, depurative, diuretic, galactagogue , hemostatic, revulsive (see herb glossary for definitions).*

## Preservation
*The leaves should be dried at a temperature less than $35^0C$ and kept out of light in airtight containers.*

## Specifics
*To avoid skin irritation, never touch the tip of the leaves when harvesting. Nettles contain a lot of chlorophyll, which is frequently used in the making of cosmetics and soaps, food colouring, and industrial solvents, for example.*

## INGREDIENTS

- 1/2 cup (120 g) unsalted butter
- 4 back pieces of a small pike, 7 oz (210 g) each
- Salt and pepper
- 3 oz (90 g) Spanish onion, finely chopped
- 7 oz (210 g) stonecrop leaves
- 7 oz (210 g) sorrel leaves
- 1 cup (250 ml) red wine
- 10 oz (300 g) pommes de terre noisette (potato balls)
- White roux (pp. 132)
- 7 cups (210 g) parsley, chopped

# Pike Back with Nettles and Stonecrop
4 servings

*Pike back is the central cut of a fish with bones. Why choose a small pike for this recipe? Simply because pike has a lot of bones, which have the advantage of melting into the meat while it cooks. Stonecrop is everywhere in Quebec. The new leaves are crunchy, like cabbage. When cooked, it tastes like sorrel and can be a substitute for spinach.*

- With a brush, grease the bottom of a baking dish that can easily fit the pike backs. Season the inside and outside of the backs with salt and pepper and arrange them in the dish. Spread the onions, stonecrop, and sorrel around. Add the wine. Cover with a piece of parchment paper and cook in a 400°F (200°C) oven for 8 minutes. Remove the pike backs and keep warm.
- Strain the cooking liquid through a cone-shaped or fine mesh sieve and cook the potatoes in it. When they are cooked, thicken the cooking liquid with the white roux to obtain your desired consistency. Strain the liquid again through the sieve and adjust the seasoning.
- Put the pike backs onto a serving dish. Surround with the potatoes and pour the sauce on top. Sprinkle with parsley.

## Poached Eggs, Nettle Purée, and Hollandaise Sauce

4 servings

*Unsalted butter is always used because of its higher fat content.*

- To prepare the hollandaise, melt the butter.
- In a separate pot, reduce the wine, shallots, and vinegar by 90%. Strain the reduction through a lined cone-shaped or fine mesh sieve. Cool.
- In a heat-proof bowl, whisk together the egg yolks, the reduction, salt, and pepper. In a warm bain-marie, emulsify the mixture until it forms ribbons (as with whipped cream). This step is very important. Emulsifying the egg yolks with the acidity of the white wine in the bain-marie will ensure the success of the sauce.
- Drizzle in the melted butter so the mixture becomes smooth. Add the lemon juice as needed.
- Heat the olive oil in a large pot on medium heat. Drop in the nettle leaves and cook until all the moisture has evaporated. Season with salt, pepper, and set aside.
- Fill a sauté pan with water and the vinegar and bring to a boil. Break the eggs into the rolling water and cook for 4 to 5 minutes (depending on their size), to soft poach. Drain them on a kitchen towel.
- In the bottom of each dish, place small circles of nettle purée. Put an egg in each circle and top with the hollandaise sauce. Serve with the potatoes.

## INGREDIENTS

### Hollandaise Sauce

- 3/4 cup (180 g) unsalted butter
- 1/2 cup (125 ml) white wine
- 1 oz (30 g) shallots, chopped
- 2 teaspoons white vinegar
- 4 egg yolks
- Salt and white pepper
- Juice of half of a lemon (or more, depending)

- 1/2 cup (125 ml) extra-virgin olive oil
- 2 lb (1 kg) young nettle leaves, washed and drained
- Salt and pepper
- 1 tablespoon + 1 teaspoon (20 ml) white vinegar
- 8 eggs
- Small fingerling potatoes, cooked in salted water

*Curly parsley*

*Flat parsley*

# PARSLEY

Wild Variety - *Petroselinum sativum* (*Linnaeus*)
Cultivated Variety - *Petroselinum hortense* (*Linnaeus*)

The word parsley comes from the Greek, *petros selinon*, meaning "rock celery." This herb, originating in Sardinia, has been an aromatic and garnish since antiquity. The Greeks crowned the winners of games dedicated to Neptune with parsley garlands. Pliny the Elder recommended sprinkling parsley onto the surface of water to invigorate fish.

During the Roman era, this wonderful herb was found in gardens everywhere except the extreme north. Interestingly, up until the end of the Middle Ages, parsley was only grown for medicinal use.

A biannual or annual plant, parsley has dark green leaves divided into three leaflets and small greenish or yellow flowers arranged in umbels. The roots are fusiform (spindle-shaped) and the fruit is ovoid. These days, the flat variety is preferred over the curly, which is more decorative but less aromatic.

## Other Names

*Garden parsley, Italian parsley, flat parsley, curly parsley.*

## Cooking Uses

*Parsley is an indispensable part of a bouquet garni and is essential for making stocks, fumets (reductions), and essences. The subtle and delicate aroma of parsley enhances even the most bland sauces and meats. It nicely flavours herb omelettes, salads, heavy starches, and ordinary soups.*

## Therapeutic Uses

*Antiemetic, antiscorbutic, aparient, diuretic, emmenagogue, sedative, stimulant and tonic, anti-galactagogue, alternative, expectorant (see herb glossary for definitions).*

## Preservation

*Parsley dries well. It should be kept in an airtight jar away from light.*

## Specifics

*Certain cultures eat parsley to encourage passion and fertility in men as well as in women.*

## INGREDIENTS

### Stuffing

- 3 1/3 oz (100 g) chicken livers
- 3 1/3 oz (100 g) quail or chicken meat
- 3 1/3 oz (100 g) pork loin
- 2 slices of bread, soaked in 1/2 cup (125 ml) heavy cream (35%)
- 1 egg
- Cognac
- Salt and pepper
- 1/3 cup (10 g) parsley, finely chopped

- 4 oz (120 g) almonds, slivered
- 4 quails
- Salt and pepper
- 1 cup (250 ml) quail stock
- 5 cups (150 ml) parsley
- 1/2 cup (125 ml) peanut oil
- 1/2 cup (125 ml) Madeira
- 1/2 cup (125 ml) Noilly Prat vermouth
- 5 1/3 cups (160 g) mirepoix (a mixture of diced onion, celery, and carrot)
- 1/2 cup (120 g) unsalted butter

## Stuffed Quail with a Parsley Almond Jus

4 servings

- To prepare the stuffing, run all the ingredients through a meat grinder with a medium-sized disc.
- Toast the almonds in the oven at $350^0$F ($180^0$C).
- Carefully debone the quails through the back (see p. 136), making sure not to leave any bones, and season them with salt and pepper. Spread the stuffing onto the inside the quails and close them up, forming them into the shape of a quail. Set aside.
- In a blender or a food processor, emulsify the cold quail stock with the parsley. Strain the mixture through a fine sieve. Chop the almonds with a knife or in the food processor and add to the parsley mixture.
- Heat the peanut oil in a sauté pan. Add the quails, making sure they are closed, and season them with salt and pepper. Put them in the oven for 8 minutes at $350^0$F ($180^0$C) to sear them well. Lower the temperature to $285^0$F ($140^0$C) and continue to cook, basting often. Cook until the internal temperature on the thermometer reads $160^0$F ($70^0$C).
- Remove the quails from the pan and drain off the excess cooking fat. Deglaze with the Madeira, Noilly Prat, and mirepoix. Add 1 cup (250 ml) of water and cook for 5 to 6 minutes.
- Strain through a cone-shaped or fine mesh sieve and add the parsley-almond mixture. Reduce by half. Finish the jus with butter. Place each of the quails on a plate and sauce with the jus.

### Vegetables

- Fresh artichoke hearts
- Roasted potatoes or pommes parisiennes
- Mixed vegetables

## Moules Marinières

4 servings

*The importance of parsley in preparing mussels is basic, but do not overcook the parsley. Wait until the guests are seated at the table to begin cooking. To serve, use a chafing dish in the centre of the table to keep the mussels hot in their shells. They will cool too quickly if served on a plate. Give each guest a little bowl for the cooking liquid. Whitish mussels are male and the yellow ones are female.*

- The mussels need to be cooked covered, so use a large enough pot. Pour in the wine, shallots, pepper, and butter. Add the mussels. Cover and cook on high heat until they open. Stir occasionally so they open uniformly. Serve immediately and sprinkle with parsley.
- Place a few mussels in individual heated soup plates. Pour cooking liquid in small heated bowls. Each time you take a mussel from the shell, add some of the jus with a spoon.

- 1 cup (250 ml) dry white wine, such as Muscadet
- 1/2 cup (90 g) shallots, finely chopped
- Freshly ground pepper
- 1/4 cup (60 g) unsalted butter
- 2 to 3 1/3 lb (1 to 1.5 kg) small farmed mussels, washed in running water and drained
- 2 cups (60 g) parsley, finely chopped

## INGREDIENTS

- 1/4 cup (45 g) shallots, finely chopped
- 1 cup (250 ml) white wine
- 1 cup (240 ml) unsalted butter, at room temperature
- Salt and pepper
- 4 halibut steaks, 5 to 6 oz (150 to 180 g) each
- 1 cup (250 ml) olive oil
- 1 cup (30 g) parsley, chopped
- Juice of 2 limes

## Grilled Halibut with Parsley Butter and Lime Emulsion
**4 servings**

*Let the butter sit at room temperature the night before making this recipe.*

- Put the shallots, wine, 2 oz (60 g) of butter, salt, and pepper in a pot. Reduce by 90%. Cool, cover, and keep in the fridge.
- Dry the halibut steaks well. Season them with salt and pepper and brush them with 1/4 cup (60 ml) olive oil. Heat a grill pan so there are two surface temperatures—one very hot and the other medium. Make crisscross grill marks on both sides of the fish on the hot part of the grill. Move the fish to the cooler part of the grill to finish cooking it. The meat will fall away from the bones.
- While the fish is cooking, mix 6 oz (180 g) of butter with the shallots and the wine and parsley reduction. In a blender on high, mix the lime juice, salt, pepper, and the rest of the oil. Set aside.
- Place a halibut steak on each plate. Spoon a band of the lime emulsion all around the plate and cover the halibut with 1 teaspoon of parsley butter.

### Vegetables
- Steamed potatoes
- Parsnips
- Parsley root

*Rosemary*

# ROSEMARY

## *Rosmarinus officinalis* (*Linnaeus*)

### Lamiaceae Family

Rosemary, a sacred plant, was woven with bay leaves into the crowns of Roman heroes. It was part of pagan religious festivals, weddings, and funeral ceremonies. In the 17th century, its essence was used to prepare the original "*eau de la reine de Hongrie*," (perfume of the Queen of Hungary), which bestowed youth, beauty, and love on the Hungarian queen, Elizabeth, well into her seventies.

Rosemary, also known as "rose of the sea," is a shrub that can reach a height of 1.5 metres and can live for 30 years. Remarkably, it flowers year round, yielding bluish flowers that release a pleasant, lightly camphorated aroma. It has a spicy, herbaceous, bitter taste. It is used in many forms: fresh, dried, whole, ground, and powdered.

## Other Names

*Compass plant, Polar plant, Rosmarinus coronarium, Garden Rosemary.*

## Cooking Uses

*When cooked, rosemary releases a unique flavour that pairs perfectly with lamb, some fish, soups, sausages, and cheeses. It is also used to make Italian chestnut cake (castagnaccio).*

## Therapeutic Uses

*Antidepressant, antioxidant, pulmonary antiseptic, antispasmodic, bactericidal, carminative, diaphoretic, diuretic, emmenagogue, fungicide, hypertensor, nervous system stimulant, circulatory stimulant, vascular tonic (see herb glossary for definitions). It also helps treat baldness.*

## Preservation

*Rosemary should be protected from the cold in winter. The leaves are picked in summer and dried at less than 35°C.*

## Specifics

*In the Middle Ages, rosemary branches were burnt in hospital hallways to sterilize the air. Rosemary was used by those who practised white magic for love, protection, purification, and memory. To attract love, wash your hands with a rosemary infusion.*

## INGREDIENTS

- 5 oz (150 g) sliced white bread, without the crust
- 1/2 cup (125 ml) heavy cream (35%)
- 13 oz (400 g) lean ground lamb
- 1 oz (30 g) rosemary, powdered
- 1/2 onion, finely chopped
- 1 clove of garlic, finely chopped
- 1 juniper berry, powdered
- 1/2 cup (15 g) parsley, finely chopped
- 1 egg white
- Salt and pepper

- 1 lamb shoulder, 2 1/2 to 3 1/3 lb (1.2 to 1.5 kg)
- Pork caul fat (optional)
- 2/3 cup (150 ml) peanut oil
- 5 oz (150 g) mirepoix (diced onion, carrot, celery)
- 2/3 cup (150 ml) brown lamb stock or store-bought demi-glace

# Lamb Shoulder Stuffed with Rosemary

4 to 8 servings

*Ask your butcher to debone the lamb shoulder. Make sure you also get the bones cut into small cubes and the lean meat for the stuffing ground with a medium disc. Caul fat is the fatty, transparent membrane around pork or veal stomach and organs (see note p. 18).*

- To prepare the stuffing, soak the bread in the cream and finely chop in the food processor. Mix together the lamb, soaked bread, rosemary, onions, garlic, juniper, parsley, and egg white. Season with salt and pepper.
- Season the inside of the lamb shoulder with salt and pepper. Stuff with the lamb and herb mixture and close up. Wrap the shoulder in the pork caul fat or tie with butcher's twine.
- Heat oil in a baking dish and brown the stuffed lamb shoulder on all sides. Place the cubes of bone all around. Cook in the oven at 400°F (200°C), basting often, until the internal temperature reads 130°F (55°C) on a thermometer. At this point, remove the cooking fat from the pan. Add the mirepoix and lamb stock. When the thermometer reads 150°F (65°C), remove the lamb shoulder from the oven and keep it warm.
- Stir the cooking liquid and strain through a lined cone-shaped or fine seive. Adjust the seasoning and set aside. Pour the lamb jus in the bottom of the plates and place slices of the stuffed shoulder on top. Always serve the sauce with the meat to maintain all the flavours.

Vegetables

- Flageolets (white beans) with waxed beans
- Flageolets (white beans) with green beans
- Mashed potatoes

# Roast Pork with Maple Gastrique and Rosemary Sauce

**4 servings**

*A gastrique is a reduction, to the point of caramelization, of vinegar or fruit juice and sugar with added aromatics. Be careful when adding the cold water as the caramel is very hot and can splash. Wearing gloves is recommended to avoid burns. The tenderloin is the spine of the pork. This part of the meat has a bit more fat, but it is so much tastier.*

- To prepare the gastrique, pour the maple syrup and vinegar into a pot and cook on high heat until caramelized. Stop the cooking immediately by carefully pouring in cold water to obtain a nice golden colour.
- Make incisions in the roast and stuff with the pieces of garlic. Season with salt and pepper.
- Heat the oil in a Dutch oven and sear the pork roast. Cook in the oven at 400$^0$F (200$^0$C), basting often. When the thermometer reads an internal temperature of 150$^0$F (65$^0$C), add the onions, carrots, and celery to the roast. Continue cooking until the internal temperature reaches 160$^0$F (70$^0$C). Remove the roast and keep it warm. Remove the excess fat from the pot. Pour in the maple gastrique and add the rosemary. Cook for a few minutes and strain the jus through a mesh sieve.
- Pour some jus into each plate and place thick slices of the roast on top.

## Rosemary Oil

- At the end of summer, put two sprigs of rosemary with leaves into a bottle. Cover with olive oil. Macerate for several months.

## INGREDIENTS

- 1 1/4 cups (300 ml) maple syrup
- 1 cup (250 ml) white wine vinegar
- Pork loin roast 2 to 2 1/2 lb (1 to 1.2 kg)
- 4 cloves of garlic, peeled and sliced lengthwise into thin slices
- Salt and pepper
- 1/4 cup (60 ml) peanut oil
- 1 onion, diced for mirepoix
- 1 carrot, diced for mirepoix
- 1 celery stalk, diced for mirepoix
- 50 g rosemary, powdered

### Vegetables
- Mashed potatoes
- Artichoke hearts with peas

*Sage*

*Pineapple Sage*

*Fruit Sage*

*Clary Sage*

# SAGE

## Salvia officinalis (*Linnaeus*)

### Lamiaceae Family

Known since the time of Hippocrates, sage has an exceptional reputation. Its name, derived from the Latin *salvare*, means "to protect." In the fourteenth century, the poet Salerno sang this famous verse: "But who can write thy worth, (O sovereign Sage!). Some ask how a man can die where thou dost grow." Sage is also mentioned in connection with longevity in an old proverb: "Whoever wishes to live forever must eat sage in May."

The shrub reaches a height of 1 metre. Its purplish-blue, sometimes pink, flowers are grouped in spikes. Harvested twice a year, sage leaves are dried away from light, at a temperature below 35⁰C. The aroma is intense and distinct. The flavour is spicy, astringent, strong, and slightly bitter. Sage pairs well with garlic and onions.

## Other Names
*Garden sage, tree sage, common sage.*

## Cooking Uses
*The flavour of sage—spicy, astringent, strong, and slightly bitter—is not to everyone's taste. However, it goes well with grilled tuna, eel, mutton, lamb, veal, pork chops, stuffing, and some vegetables.*

## Therapeutic Uses
*Internal usages: tonic, antispasmodic, antiseptic, diuretic, hypertensor, emmenagogue, antisudorific, anti-galactagogue, estrogenic, carminative, antioxidant.*

*External usages: astringent, cicatrizant, antiseptic, antirheumatism tonic (see herb glossary for definitions).*

## Preservation
*The leaves are dried, out of light, at a temperature lower than 35⁰C. The aroma is intense and distinct.*

## Specifics
*Sage sanitizes closets and linens. Sage tea, when taken regularly one month before childbirth, considerably reduces pain. It is also the basis of many Native rituals.*

## INGREDIENTS

### Tapenade

- 8 oz (240 g) black olives, pitted
- 3 1/3 oz (100 g) canned anchovy fillets, drained
- 3 1/3 oz (100 g) canned tuna, drained
- 3 1/3 oz (100 g) capers, drained
- 1 sprig of thyme
- 2 teaspoons (10 g) sage leaves
- 1/4 bay leaf
- 2 garlic cloves, peeled
- 3 tablespoons Cognac
- 2/3 cup (150 ml) olive oil
- Black pepper

- 4 veal chops, 6 to 7 oz (180 to 210 g) each, bone in
- Salt and pepper
- 1/3 cup (75 ml) peanut oil
- 1/2 cup (125 ml) white wine
- 1/4 cup (45 g) shallots, finely chopped
- 2/3 cup (150 ml) light veal stock
- 1/2 cup (120 g) unsalted butter

## Veal Chops with Sage Tapenade

4 servings

*Tapenade was invented by a Monsieur Meynier of Marseille. Its name comes from* tapeno, *a provincial name for "capers," an ingredient that is often overlooked.*

- Except for the olive oil and pepper, blend all the ingredients for the tapenade in the food processor. When a smooth purée is obtained, add the oil and pepper. Keep in the fridge in an airtight container to maintain the flavours, but remember that tapenade should always be served at room temperature.
- Season the veal chops with salt and pepper. Heat the peanut oil in a heavy-bottom pan and sear the veal chops on each side. Lower the temperature and cook until you get an internal temperature of $160^0$F ($70^0$C). Remove chops from the pan and keep warm.
- Remove the excess cooking fat and deglaze with the wine and shallots. Reduce by 90% and add the veal stock. Cook for 1 minute and finish with butter. Adjust the seasoning.
- Place a chop on each plate. Top with 1 tablespoon of the tapenade and spoon a band of jus around the plate.

### Vegetables
- Potato gratin
- Green beans
- Cauliflower

# Mackerel Fillets with Sage and White Wine
### 4 servings

*To flute, means to hollow out small, shallow V-shaped grooves with a lemon zester for decoration. This recipe is perfect for the summer season.*

- To prepare the court-bouillon, put the lemon, carrots, onions, garlic, wine, bouquet garni, sage, clove, peppercorns, and salt in a pot. Cook slowly for 20 minutes until all the ingredients are cooked and have an acidic flavour. Set aside.
- While the court-bouillon is cooking, place the mackerel fillets on a baking dish, skin side down. Pour the warm court-bouillon over the fillets, cover with a piece of parchment paper and cook in the oven at 350°F (180°C) for 12 to 18 minutes, until they are firm.
- Keep in the fridge for at least 12 hours. Serve very cold with a green salad or boiled potatoes.

## INGREDIENTS

### Court-Bouillon

- 1 lemon, fluted and cut into thin slices
- 1 carrot, fluted and cut into thin slices
- 1 Spanish onion, cut into thin slices
- 1 garlic clove
- 1 cup (250 ml) white wine
- 1 bouquet garni
- 1/3 oz (10 g) sage leaves, chopped
- 1/2 clove
- 10 black peppercorns
- Salt
- 8 mackerel fillets

## INGREDIENTS

- 1 chicken, 3 1/3 to 4 lb (1.5 to 1.8 kg)
- 1/2 oxtail, cut into 1" (2.5 cm) pieces
- 2 leeks, white part only
- 4 celery stalks
- 4 tomatoes, cut in two and seeded
- 2 onions, spiked with 2 cloves
- 3 sprigs of sage
- 6 carrots
- 1/2 head of garlic
- 1 2/3 cups (400 ml) white wine
- 10 black peppercorns
- Dill pickles
- Strong mustard
- Coarse sea salt

## Chicken and Beef Hotchpotch with a Sage Broth

4 to 8 servings

*Hotchpotch is a boiled pot-au-feu from Flanders, traditionally made with beef or mutton, which may also contain oxtails, among other things.* The Agronomist (The Farmer's Portable Dictionary), *published in 1760, also gives the name Hotchpotch to chicken cooked with oxtails. It is important to use chicken for this recipe, as the cooking broth is as important as the meat.*

- Put the chicken and the oxtail into a large pot and top with water. Bring it to a boil and skim.
- Wash the leeks and celery well and tie them together. Add the tomatoes, onions, leeks, celery, sage, carrots, garlic, wine, and pepper to the pot. Simmer slowly for about 1 hour at 206°F (95°C), until the oxtails and the chicken are cooked.
- Remove the vegetables from the broth and keep them warm. Remove and cut the chicken and oxtail into same size pieces and arrange them in a deep serving dish. Surround with the vegetables and cover to keep warm.
- Give each person a cup of broth and a very hot soup plate for the meat and vegetables, accompanied by dill pickles, strong mustard, and coarse sea salt.

### Vegetables

- Halfway through cooking the chicken, at the same time as you add the vegetables to the pot, you can also begin to cook some potatoes.

*Summer Savory*

# SAVORY

Savory - *Satureja hortensis* (*Linnaeus*) | Winter Savory - *Satureja montana* (*Linnaeus*)

Lamiaceae Family

Virgil sang about savory, as did Martial, who, in an epigram that reproached Lupercus for his impotence, insisted that even the supposed aphrodisiac qualities of savory could not help the poor soul. In the Middle Ages, savory was called *saturiam* and had an honoured place in monastic chapter houses.

An annual plant, with a woody stalk reaching 20 to 30 centimetres in height, savory grows close to the ground. It has strong branches with linear, oblong, fragrant downy leaves. It possesses a short petiole with small white or purplish pink flowers.

## Other Names
*Summer savory, Winter savory.*

## Cooking Uses
*Finely chopped, savory goes well with sage in salads. It is used to wrap ewe's milk cheese. A branch of savory is recommended when cooking lentils and beans to prevent gas and bloating. Savory is used in some stuffings, and it is an important part of the exquisite herb mixture, herbes de provence. It is very useful in minimizing the strong flavour of game meats by neutralizing the active effect of the toxins.*

## Therapeutic Uses
*Digestive, brain and adrenal cortex stimulant, antispasmodic, carminative, antiseptic, vermifuge, expectorant (see herb glossary for definitions). St. Hildegard and St. Albert the Great recommended it for gout.*

## Preservation
*Savory does not dry well and, in powdered form, it loses its flavour over time.*

## Specifics
*Savory goes well with basil and chervil in an herb mixture called "herbes à tortue" (literally, turtle grass). It is used in the making of Chartreuse and is superb when combined with lemon balm in cordials.*

## Scallops Poached in Almond Milk with a Savory Emulsion
4 servings

*Do not confuse scallops with coquilles St. Jacques. There are no coquilles St. Jacques in Quebec. Scallops are bivalve molluscs from the Pectinidae family. There are many varieties, from small and tender bay scallops to giant scallops with flavourful flesh. It is easy to obtain coquilles St. Jacques in Europe where they are found in the Atlantic and the Mediterranean.*

- Spread out the scallops on a towel. Season them with salt and pepper on both sides.
- Heat the almond milk to $175^0$F ($80^0$C) and add the scallops. The temperature should not exceed $175^0$F ($80^0$C). If cooked this way, scallops will not toughen. To ensure the scallops are cooked, the temperature should read $145^0$F ($62^0$C). Remove the scallops immediately and set aside.
- In a blender, mix the egg yolks, savory, and lemon juice at high speed. Drizzle in 1/4 cup (60 ml) of the almond milk and season with salt and pepper to taste. Sauce the scallops with the emulsion and serve.

## INGREDIENTS

- 16 scallops (12/15 per kg)
- Salt and white pepper
- 1 cup (250 ml) almond milk
- 2 egg yolks
- 1 cup (30 g) savory, finely chopped
- Juice of one lemon

## INGREDIENTS

### Provençale

- 1/2 slice of bread, diced, with crusts removed
- 1 bay leaf
- 1 tsp (5 g) dried rosemary
- 1 tsp (5 g) dried thyme
- 1 tsp (5 g) dried marjoram
- 1 tsp (5 g) dried savory
- Rounded 1/2 tsp (3 g) dried sage
- Rounded 1/2 tsp (3 g) dried basil
- 1 tsp (5 g) tarragon
- 2 cloves of garlic

- 2 racks of lamb
- Salt and pepper
- 3 1/3 oz (100 g) lamb fat, taken from the racks
- 2/3 cup (150 ml) Dijon mustard
- 1/2 cup (150 ml) dry white wine
- 3 1/3 oz (100 g) unsalted butter

## Rack of Lamb Provençale
**4 servings**

*Ask your butcher to prepare the rack of lamb. If you don't use all the provençale (herbes de provence), keep it in the fridge in an airtight container.*

- To prepare the *provençale*, process the bread in a food processor. Add the aromatic herbs and the garlic and pulse for 1 to 2 minutes.
- Season the lamb racks with salt and pepper. In a large oven-proof pan, melt the lamb fat and sear the lamb racks. Put them into the oven at 400⁰F (200⁰C) for 4 to 6 minutes, depending on the thickness of the meat. Remove the racks from the pan. Brush the inside and outside with mustard. Cover the outside only with the *provençale*. Raise the temperature of the oven to broil. Put the racks in the oven. When a crust forms on the racks, they are perfectly cooked.
- While the lamb racks are in the oven, remove the excess fat from the pan. Pour in the wine, reduce by 90%, and add 3/4 cup (200 ml) water. Reduce again by a quarter, finish with butter, and sprinkle in 2 tablespoons of the *provençale*. Adjust the seasoning. Pour some jus into the bottom of each plate and cut the beautiful lamb chops into individual portions.

### Vegetables

- Pommes de terre boulangères
- Gratin dauphinois
- Green beans
- Flageolets (white beans)

## Pheasant Supremes with Savory Wine

4 servings

*You can start preparing this dish the night before. Female pheasant is generally more tender than the male. Your butcher can separate the supremes (breasts) from the thighs. Make sure to keep the carcass, which you will need to make the quick pheasant stock. Also, ask your butcher to vacuum pack the thighs. You can keep them in the freezer for another use.*

- Season the supremes with salt and pepper. Heat oil in a heavy-bottom pan and quickly sear the supremes to brown. Remove from the pan and cool. In another pan, place the supremes, carrots, onions, celery, bouquet garni, and garlic. Cover with the savory wine. Leave on the counter for 24 hours, covered.
- The next day, pour everything into a pot and add the pheasant stock. Cook at 205°F (95°C) for about 20 minutes. The internal temperature of the supremes should be 162°F (72°C). Remove the supremes and keep warm. Strain the liquid and thicken it with the white roux to your liking. Put the supremes into the sauce and serve very hot.

## Quick Pheasant Stock

*Get your butcher to cut the pheasant carcass into small pieces.*

- Heat the oil in a sauté pan and brown the pieces of pheasant carcass until they are a dark golden brown.
- Remove the fat; add the shallots, carrots, celery, and wine. Cook for 2 to 3 minutes to remove the acidity of the wine and cover with water. Cook for 20 minutes and make sure all the bones remain covered with liquid.
- Strain through a cone-shaped sieve or a mesh strainer. The stock is ready to use.

### Vegetables
- Wild Rice
- Mixed spring vegetables

## INGREDIENTS

- 2 pheasant supremes (breasts)
- Salt and pepper
- 1/4 cup (60 ml) peanut oil
- 1 carrot, diced for mirepoix
- 1 onion, diced for mirepoix
- 1 celery stalk, diced for mirepoix
- 1 bouquet garni
- 2 cloves of garlic
- 3 cups (750 ml) savory wine (p.111)
- 1 cup (250 ml) brown pheasant stock or store-bought demi-glace
- Cold white roux (p. 132)

---

- 1/2 cup (125 ml) oil
- Pheasant carcass in small pieces
- 2 shallots, minced
- 1/2 carrot, minced
- 1/2 celery stalk, minced
- 1 cup (250 ml) white wine

## INGREDIENTS

- 10 oz (300 g) savory, washed and dried
- 2/3 oz (20 g) juniper
- 3 1/3 oz (100 g) tansy, washed and dried
- 1 cup (250 ml) 45% alcohol
- 3 cups (750 ml) dry white wine

## Savory Wine

*At the end of summer, you can make herb wines that will last you through the winter. Herb wine can be used to deglaze meat or fish, infusing it with the flavour of savory. Tansy is a wild plant with yellow flowers that has been used forever to eliminate parasites. Pregnant women should not touch or consume this plant. Easy to grow, tansy is not well known, except among botanists. Also called golden buttons, it is excellent in omelettes and puddings.*

- Put the savory, juniper, and tansy in a wide-mouth jar. Cover with the alcohol and wine. Allow to macerate for 3 to 10 days in a cupboard. Decant and pass through a coffee filter. If the liquid remains cloudy, add 1 teaspoon of egg white. Shake well.
- Let it sit for 24 hours. Decant and filter again. Age it for a few months in a cupboard.

*Sorrel*

*Common sorrel*

*Mountain sorrel*

# SORREL

## *Rumex acetosa*

### Polygonaceae Family

Originating in northern Asia, sorrel somewhat resembles spinach, even if it is not part of the same botanical family. The ancients seem to have totally ignored it, but it was used in the Middle Ages to lend fragrance to sauces for game meats.

Sorrel is a perennial plant measuring 30 centimetres to 1 metre in height. Its stalk is reddish, ribbed, hollow, and branched. The large leaves are dark green on the bottom and bluish-grey on top, arrow-shaped, clasping, and they produce auricles. The flowers are green or reddish.

## Other Names
*Common sorrel, garden sorrel.*

## Cooking Uses
*Sorrel is very acidic due to its exposure to the sun. It goes very well with many different kinds of fish, enhancing the flavour. It belongs among the great classics of cuisine (cream of sorrel, salads, chicken broth, and vegetable dishes, etc.).*

## Therapeutic Uses
*Antiscorbutic, aparient, diuretic, emmenagogue, refreshing stomachic, tonic (see herb glossary for definitions).*

## Preservation
*Sorrel should be cooked, then frozen or vacuum sealed.*

## Specifics
*In* The Mysterious Island *by Jules Verne, the shipwrecked sailors were delighted to discover that the sorrel plant could cure scurvy. Never cook sorrel in an aluminum pot and use a steel knife to cut it.*

## INGREDIENTS

- 16 to 20 cups (4 to 5 L) salted water
- 5 oz (150 g) spinach leaves
- 5 oz (150 g) sorrel leaves
- 5 oz (150 g) Swiss chard leaves
- 5 oz (150 g) Boston lettuce leaves
- 5 oz (150 g) chicory leaves
- 5 oz (150 g) young Savoy cabbage leaves
- 3 oz (90 g) duck fat
- 1 Spanish onion, minced
- 1 clove of garlic, finely chopped
- Salt and pepper
- 2 eggs
- 2/3 cup (150 ml) milk
- 1 cup (30 g) chervil sprigs

## Herb Gratin
4 servings

*Only the leaves, not the ribs of the vegetables should be used in this recipe. This gratin pairs well with fish, lamb, beef, and poultry.*

- Heat the salt water in a large pot. Very quickly blanch the spinach, sorrel, chard, lettuce, chicory, and the Savoy cabbage. Shock immediately in cold water to stop the cooking. Drain and press the mixture between your hands to extract the maximum amount of water. Chop finely with a knife and set aside.
- In a pot, heat the duck fat on medium heat and sweat the onions and garlic. Add the herbs, salt, and pepper. Remove from the heat. Lightly beat the eggs and milk together. Pour this into the pot while stirring.
- Pour into a baking dish and cook in the oven at 400°F (200°C), until the dish is cooked *au gratin* (brown on top). Sprinkle with the chervil and serve immediately.

## Shad with Sorrel

**4 servings**

*This is a wonderful recipe from my grandmother. Shad is a relative of herring. The meat is so delicate that it was given the nickname "Atlantic tenderloin." This fish is succulent, but if the bones have not been softened, it can be tricky to eat.*

- Put the shad in a sauté pan after making crisscross incisions 1/2" (1 cm) deep on each side. Season with salt and pepper and pour the oil over the fish. Cover with plastic wrap and keep in the fridge.
- Heat the salted water, add the leek and cook for 20 minutes. Remove the leek with a slotted spoon and add the sorrel. Cook for 1 to 2 minutes. Drain. When the sorrel has cooled, remove the excess liquid by pressing it between your hands; put it in the sauté pan with the leeks. At the same time, heat the milk and thicken it with the white roux to obtain a thick sauce. Add the egg yolks, sorrel, and leeks. Adjust the seasoning and serve hot.
- Heat a grill pan and make sure there are two cooking areas—one very hot, the other medium hot. On the hottest part of the grill, sear the shad, giving it crisscross grill marks on each side. Move the fish to the cooler part of the grill to continue cooking until the bones come away from the meat. Serve very hot with the sorrel purée.

### Vegetables
- Steamed potatoes

## INGREDIENTS

- 1 spring shad, about 4 1/2 to 5 1/2 lb (2 to 2.5 kg), cleaned well and dried
- Salt and pepper
- 1/2 cup (125 ml) sunflower oil
- 4 cups (1 L) salted water
- 1/2 leek, minced
- 2 lb (1 kg) sorrel leaves
- 2 cups (500 ml) milk
- White roux (p. 132)
- 2 egg yolks, beaten

## INGREDIENTS

- 1/4 cup (45 g) pearl barley
- 1/2 cup (120 g) unsalted butter
- 12 oz (360 g) sorrel leaves
- 4 cups (1 L) milk
- Salt and pepper
- 1 cup (100 g) barley flour
- Cream (15%), hot

## Sorrel and Barley Soup
### 4 servings

- Cook the barley in a bit of salted water. Rinse in cool water, drain, and set aside.
- Heat the butter in a pot. Steam the sorrel in the butter until it becomes a purée.
- Heat 3 cups (750 ml) milk and season it with salt and pepper. Mix the barley flour with the rest of the cold milk. Add this to the hot milk mixture, stirring constantly. Bring to a boil. Simmer gently for about 30 minutes. Add the sorrel purée, setting aside 4 teaspoons for garnish. Simmer for about 10 minutes and strain through a lined cone-shaped sieve. Add the cream to give it a creamy texture.
- Divide the pearl barley and the sorrel puree equally into the bottom of each dish. Drizzle in the hot soup. Garnish with the remaining sorrel purée.

*Tarragon*

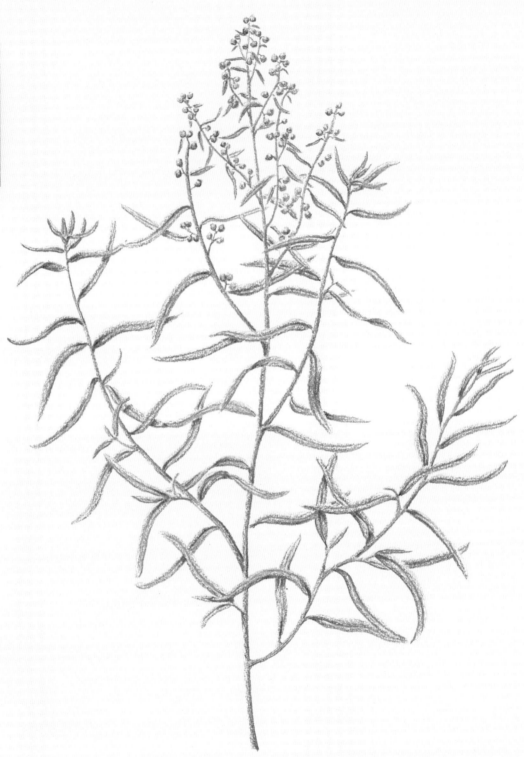

# TARRAGON

## Artemisia dracunculus (Linnaeus)

### Asteraceae Family

Tarragon originated in southern Russia and Siberia. It was widely appreciated by the Arabic people, who called it *tarkhoum*, before it won over the West—possibly by way of the Mongolian invasions, but more likely during the Crusades in the 12th century. In the 13th and 14th centuries, it was given the name *targon*, which meant "little dragon."

Tarragon is a perennial shrub that can reach 120 centimetres in height. The stalk is branched; the leaves are green and lanceolate with tiny greenish flowers grouped in capitulae. Tarragon releases a strongly aromatic, delicately spicy anise scent.

## Other Names

*Little dragon, French Tarragon, German Tarragon, Dragon Wormwood, Dragonwort, Dragon Mugwort.*

## Cooking Uses

*The tender fresh leaves are used to flavour a number of dishes and sauces. However, the herbaceous, slightly anisette flavour of tarragon is unique and isn't to everyone's taste. Indispensable in béarnaise sauce, tarragon is also excellent in vinegar.*

## Therapeutic Uses

*General stimulant and digestive, internal antiseptic, carminative, emmenagogue, vermifuge (see herb glossary for definitions).*

## Preservation

*The leaves can be kept frozen in cubes or blanched and kept in small plastic bags in the freezer. Tarragon stands up well to drying, retaining its fragrance.*

## Specifics

*Tarragon helps curb the monotony of no-salt diets. In India, a tarragon-based mixture with fennel juice was a favourite drink of the maharajahs.*

## Tarragon Liqueur

Makes 4 cups (1 L)

- Put the tarragon, vanilla, and sugar into a glass jar. Pour in the alcohol, close with an airtight lid, and let macerate in a cupboard for one month, stirring from time to time.
- Strain and bottle.

- 3/4 cup (30 g) tarragon leaves
- 1 vanilla pod
- 1 oz (30 g) sugar
- 4 cups (1 L) alcohol, 45% proof

## INGREDIENTS

- 4 guinea fowl supremes (breasts)

### Stuffing

- 3 slices of white bread
- 1/2 cup (125 ml) heavy cream (35%)
- 2 Guinea fowl thighs, boned
- 5 oz (150 g) pork loin or pork shoulder
- 3 1/3 oz (100 g) veal
- Salt and pepper
- 1 egg
- 2 tablespoons (30 g) potato starch
- 1/4 cup (60 ml) Cognac
- 1/2 cup (20 g) tarragon leaves, finely chopped

### Sauce

- 2/3 cup (150 ml) dry white wine
- 1/2 cup (90 g) shallots, finely chopped
- 2/3 cup (150 g) unsalted butter
- 1 cup (250 ml) thickened brown poultry stock or store-bought demi-glace
- 1/2 cup (125 ml) heavy cream (35%)
- 1/2 cup (20 g) tarragon leaves, finely chopped

## Stuffed Guinea Fowl Supremes with Tarragon Cream
4 servings

*I recommend checking the taste of the stuffing before using it. To do this, make a little patty and pan-fry it. When you've tasted it, you can assess and adjust the seasoning and texture.*

- Soak the bread in 1/2 cup (125 ml) of cream.
- To make the stuffing, use a meat grinder with a medium cutting disc. Run the Guinea fowl thighs, pork, veal, and the soaked bread through the grinder twice.
- Mix well and season with salt and pepper to taste. Add the egg, potato starch, Cognac, and half the tarragon. Set aside in the fridge for at least 1 hour.
- Spread the stuffing uniformly onto the open breasts. Roll using plastic wrap and set aside.
- In a pot large enough to cook the supremes, heat the water to 205°F (95°C). Place the supremes in the water and cook until the thermometer reads an internal temperature of 167°F (75°C).
- While the supremes are cooking, make the sauce by reducing the wine and shallots in another pot. Add the butter and thickened poultry stock and cook 3 to 4 minutes. Add the cream and tarragon. Adjust the seasoning and serve very hot.

### Vegetables

- A mix of white and wild rice
- Fiddleheads
- Crosnes (also called Chinese artichoke)
- Celery root purée

## INGREDIENTS

- 4 sprigs of tarragon
- Butter
- 1/2 cup (90 g) shallots, finely chopped
- Salt and pepper
- 12 monkfish medallions, 2 oz (60 g) each
- 2/3 cup (150 ml) dry white wine
- 1 cup (250 ml) fish fumet (reduced stock) (p. 131)
- 1 cup (250 ml) heavy cream (35%)
- 2/3 cup (150 g) unsalted butter

---

- 4 1/2 lb (2 kg) pickling cucumbers
- Coarse salt
- 12 cups (3 L) white vinegar
- 4 tablespoons salt
- 6 sprigs of tarragon
- 8 cloves of garlic

## Monkfish Medallions with Tarragon

4 servings

- Strip the leaves off the sprigs of tarragon, finely chop, and cut the stalks in small pieces. Brush butter on the bottom of a baking dish and sprinkle with shallots. Season the medallions with salt and pepper on both sides and arrange them in the bottom of the dish. Pour in the wine and fish fumet, sprinkle with tarragon, cover, and put in the oven at 350°F (180°C) for 6 minutes. Remove the fish and place on paper towels. Keep warm. Reduce the cooking liquid by 90% and add the cream. Reduce again to desired consistency and finish with butter. Adjust the seasoning. Place the medallions on plates and top with the tarragon sauce.

### Vegetables

- Boiled potatoes or rice

## Cornichons

Yields 4 1/2 lb (2 kg)

- Cut the stems off the cucumbers, brush them thoroughly, and rub them in a bag of coarse salt. Wash well and drain.
- Put the cucumbers in a large bowl and cover them with white vinegar. Cover and let them macerate at room temperature for 2 to 3 days. Drain and boil the vinegar to reduce it by a third. Add the cucumbers and bring to a boil. Pour immediately into a ceramic crock and cover.
- Five days later, put the cucumbers and vinegar back on the heat; add the salt, tarragon, and garlic. When it comes to the boil, pour the cucumbers, vinegar, and the aromatics into airtight jars.

*Thyme*

*Lemon thyme*

*Common thyme*

*Creeping thyme*

# THYME

*Thymus vulgaris (Linnaeus)*

Lamiaceae Family

Greatly sought after in antiquity, thyme was used by the Egyptians to embalm mummies. The Greeks burned it as incense during sacrifices, and the Romans used it to flavour cheeses and as medication.

There are a hundred varieties of thyme. It is a small, greyish shrub that produces compact tufts with many branches. Often, it grows more than twenty centimetres off the ground. Blossoming yields small lilac-pink flowers. It is an indispensable aromatic in cooking. Creeping thyme (wild thyme) has the same therapeutic benefits as common thyme.

## Other Names
*Common thyme, garden thyme.*

## Cooking Uses
*Thyme is a key ingredient in bouquet garni. It goes well with lamb, in marinades, and is an essential ingredient in Mediterranean food (ratatouille, ragouts, eggplant, zucchini, and some cheeses).*

## Therapeutic Uses
*Diaphoretic, expectorant, deodorant, mucolytic, antitussitive.*

*Internal usage: general physical and psychic stimulant, nervous system tonic, hypertensor, expectorant, internal antiseptic, pulmonary, genitourinary, diuretic, carminative.*

*External usage: antirheumatism, cicatrizant, muscular relaxant, rubefacient (see herb glossary for definitions).*

## Preservation
*Thyme stands up well to drying. At the end of summer, hang it upside down using thread in a ventilated area until all moisture has evaporated. Keep it in a jar, tightly closed and away from light.*

## Specifics
*Anatomists named the thymus gland in the upper chest after thyme because of its physical resemblance to the leaf.*

## INGREDIENTS

- 1/3 cup (75 ml) olive oil
- 2 shallots, finely chopped
- 1 1/4 cups (300 ml) poultry stock
- *Sel de Guérande* (sea salt)
- Freshly ground pepper
- 2 fennel bulbs, cut in half
- 2 sprigs of thyme
- Tomato sauce (optional)

### Stuffing

- 8 oz (240 g) lean veal
- 8 oz (240 g) pork (tip of the tenderloin)
- 1 lb (480 g) fat back
- 3 teaspoons (15 g) salt
- 1/2 teaspoon (2 g) pepper
- 2 teaspoons (10 g) thyme leaves, chopped

### Pâté

- 1 1/2 lb (700 g) homemade or store-bought short crust pastry
- Flour
- 4 veal escalopes
- 7 oz (210 g) ham, sliced
- 2 egg yolks
- Brown veal stock

## Braised Fennel with Shallots and Thyme
4 servings

- Heat the olive oil in a pot and cook the shallots until they turn a light gold. Add the chicken stock and season with salt and pepper. Arrange the pieces of fennel side by side and sprinkle with thyme.
- Cover the pot and cook on low heat until the fennel is tender. Baste occasionally. Serve as is or with tomato sauce.

## Veal and Ham Pâté with Thyme
4 to 8 servings

- Put all the ingredients for the stuffing through the meat grinder twice, using a medium disc. Mix well and set aside.
- On a piece of plastic wrap, roll out the pastry in a rectangle 1" (2.5 cm) thick. Spread stuffing onto the pastry, leaving a 1" (2.5 cm) border all the way around.
- Flour the veal escalopes, place them on the stuffing, and spread a bit more of the stuffing on top. Place the ham slices on top of the stuffing. Cover with the rest of the stuffing and roll it up nice and tight, using the plastic wrap.
- Beat the egg yolks with a bit of water and brush the outside of the dough, making sure to seal the edges well. Keep in the fridge for 1 hour.
- Preheat the oven to 400°F (200°C) and brush the roll with the egg wash again. With the tip of a knife, make a hole on top, for the steam to escape, and bake in the oven for 50 to 60 minutes. Cut into thick slices and serve with the brown veal stock.

### Vegetables
- Carrots
- Parsnips

## Boneless Rib Steak with Onion and Thyme Relish
4 servings

- To make the relish, chop the onion, garlic, and thyme in the food processor. Heat 1/2 cup (120 g) of butter in a pot and slowly cook the onions, garlic, and thyme, covered, until all the liquid has evaporated. Season with salt, pepper, and set aside.
- Season the steaks with salt and pepper. In a large cast-iron pan, heat the oil and the rest of the butter. Sear and cook the steaks to your liking. Remove them from the pan. Allow them rest for 5 minutes in the oven.
- Remove the excess cooking fat from the pan and deglaze with the wine. Reduce 90% and add the relish. Serve the steaks on individual plates and top with the relish.

### Vegetables
- Pan-roasted potatoes, noisettes
- Parisiennes rissolées (potatoes, fried then browned in the oven)
- Green beans

## Garlic Thyme Soup
4 servings

- Cook the carrots, zucchini, and celery in 2/3 cup (150 ml) chicken stock. Drain and set aside.
- Reduce the cream by half. Cook the garlic in 2 1/3 cups (600 ml) chicken stock. Vigorously pulse in a blender, add the cream, salt, and pepper.
- Thicken with a mixture of potato starch thinned out with a bit of water to the preferred consistency. Right before serving, add the diced vegetables and sprinkle with chervil.

## INGREDIENTS

- 2 Spanish onions
- 2 cloves of garlic, chopped
- 1/3 oz (10 g) thyme leaves
- 2/3 cup (150 g) unsalted butter
- *Sel de Guérande* (sea salt)
- Freshly ground pepper

- 4 boneless rib steaks, 5 oz (150g) each
- 1/2 cup (125 ml) peanut oil
- 1 cup (250 ml) white wine

- 2 carrots, finely diced
- 2 zucchinis, finely diced
- 1 celery stalk, finely diced
- 3 cups (750 ml) chicken stock
- 1 2/3 cups (400 ml) heavy cream (35%)
- 8 cloves of garlic, minced, with the centre sprout removed
- Salt and pepper
- Potato starch
- Chervil for garnish

## Basic Recipes
### Light Poultry Stock

- 4 1/2 lbs (2 kg) poultry bones
- 1 1/2 cups (300 g) carrots, chopped medium size
- 1 cup (200 g) onions, chopped medium size
- 1/2 cup (100 g) leeks, white part only, chopped medium size
- 1/2 cup (100 g) celery, chopped medium size
- 3 cloves of garlic, chopped
- 1 clove
- Black pepper
- 1 bouquet garni: 20 parsley stems + 1 spring of thyme + 1/2 bay leaf

- Soak the poultry bones. Drain. Put the vegetables, garlic, and the seasonings into a stock pot with the soaked bones. Cover with water and bring to a boil. Skim, if necessary. Add the bouquet garni. Simmer for 45 minutes. Strain through a lined cone-shaped sieve or a fine mesh strainer. Reduce if the taste isn't strong enough.

### Vegetable Essence

*Vegetable essence is a concentration of flavours extracted from one or more ingredients. For example, you can make a celery essence. You can also make a mixed vegetable essence. Simply cook the base ingredient(s) in water and, after cooking, reduce the liquid to concentrate the flavours.*

### Brown Poultry Stock

- 4 1/2 lbs (2 kg) poultry bones
- 2/3 cup (150 ml) vegetable oil
- 1 1/2 cups (300 g) carrots, chopped medium size
- 1 cup (200 g) onions, chopped medium size
- 1/2 cup (100 g) leeks, white part only, chopped medium size
- 1/2 cup (100 g) celery, chopped medium size
- 3 cloves of garlic, chopped
- 1 clove
- Black pepper
- 1 bouquet garni: 20 parsley stems + 1 spring of thyme + 1/2 bay leaf
- Tomato paste (optional)

- Chop the bones up with a cleaver and brown them in the oven on a cookie sheet with 1/3 cup (75 ml) oil, until they are golden. If the bones have a good colour, they will colour the stock. While the bones are browning, sweat the vegetables in the rest of the oil and put them in a stock pot. Then add the bones and seasonings. Cover with water and simmer for 45 to 60 minutes. If the stock isn't brown enough, add a bit of tomato paste. Strain through a lined cone-shaped sieve or a fine mesh strainer.

## Brown Veal Stock

*This stock isn't thick, but by adding white roux, it becomes a thickened brown stock. For a light veal stock, use the same recipe, but don't brown the bones.*

- Vegetable oil
- 22 lbs (10 kg) veal bones (preferably knees cut into small pieces by your butcher)
- Vegetable oil
- 2 lbs (1 kg) onions, roughly chopped
- 2 lbs (1 kg) carrots, roughly chopped
- 1 lb (480 g) celery stalks, cut in 2" (5 cm) pieces
- 1 head of garlic, not peeled
- 1 bay leaf
- 2 sprigs of thyme
- 7 cups (210 g) parsley
- 25 black peppercorns
- 7 oz (200 g) tomato paste

- Heat the vegetable oil in a roasting pan in the oven at 400°F (200°C). When it's nice and hot, add the veal bones and roast them until they are golden on all sides. This step is very important. The roasted liquid will give a nice colour to the veal stock.
- At the same time, in a pot that is large enough, sweat the vegetables in hot vegetable oil. Add the garlic, seasonings, and tomato paste, and cook.
- When these two steps are finished, mix the two preparations together in a large enough stock pot. Cover completely with water and simmer for at least 6 hours.
- Reducing and concentrating the liquid will give you a demi-glace, and reducing it even more will produce a veal glace.

## Court-Bouillon

*Court-bouillon is not often used, even though it is an excellent aromatic.*

- 10 cups (2.5 L) water
- 1/2 cup (125 ml) dry white wine
- 1/2 cup (125 ml) good quality white vinegar
- 1 oz (30 g) coarse salt
- 10 oz (300 g) white onions, thinly sliced
- 10 oz (300 g) carrots, thinly sliced
- 1 bouquet garni
- 10 black peppercorns

- Cook all the ingredients together until the carrots and onions are tender. If the court-bouillon is going to be used right away, leave the vegetables in. They can be a garnish for fish, mollusks, and shellfish. If it is made for later use, strain the bouillon through a lined cone-shaped sieve or a fine mesh strainer.

## Fish Fumet

*This fumet (reduced stock) keeps in the freezer for 2 to 3 months at most. Avoid using carrots when making fish fumet; they generally give a sweet taste to the broth. Never add salt to fish fumet because it often has to be reduced to get a fish reduction.*

- 1 1/2 tablespoons butter
- 1 3/4 lbs (800 g) fish bones and trimmings (preferably from flatfish)
- 1/3 cup (75 g) onions, minced
- 2/3 cup (125 ml) leeks, minced
- 2/3 cup (125 ml) celery, minced
- 6 tablespoons (90 ml) shallots, minced

- 5 oz (150 ml) mushrooms, minced
- 1/2 cup (125 ml) dry white wine
- 4 teaspoons (20 ml) lemon juice
- 4 cups (1 L) cold water
- A pinch of thyme
- 1/2 a bay leaf
- 10 peppercorns

- In a pot, heat the butter. Add the fish bones, trimmings, and all the vegetables. Sweat for 4 to 5 minutes. Moisten with wine, lemon juice, and cold water. Add the thyme, bay leaf, and pepper. Bring to a boil and simmer for 25 minutes. Strain through a cheesecloth. Cool and set aside.

## White and Brown Roux

*Using a roux is preferable to a starch as the gluten in flour thickens sauces better.*

- 1/2 cup (120 g) butter
- 1/2 cup (120 g) flour

- Melt the butter in the microwave for 20 seconds. Mix in the flour. Cook in 20-second increments, stirring well after each one. Once the roux starts to bubble, it is cooked.

## Roux Substitutes

*There are store-bought substitutes to thicken stocks and sauces. One of them is corn starch. If you use corn starch, the sauce should be served immediately. If not, it will become thin after 20 minutes. The result is the same with all starches (potato, rice, arrowroot, chestnut, etc.) The advantage of using rice or potato starch as a thickener, however, is that there is no taste.*

*These thickeners can also be found in stores under a variety of names, including "veloutine."*

# Cooking Techniques

## Braise

- Sear the meat to give it colour.
- Remove the excess fat.
- Deglaze with wine and cook to burn off the alcohol.
- Pour in the stock of your choice to cover half of the meat.
- Add aromatics.
- Cover and cook at a constant even temperature.

## Grill

- Thoroughly dry whatever is to be grilled.
- Brush lightly with oil and season with salt and pepper.
- Place the item to be grilled (skin side down for game birds) on a hot grill.
- Make crisscross grill marks by turning the item by a quarter.
- Make grill marks on the other side as well.
- Finish cooking on very low heat.

## Pan-Fry

- Place a piece of meat in a pan on the heat.
- Brown on one side.
- Turn the piece of meat over to brown the other side.
- Add a small accompanying garnish: carrots, onions, and bouquet garni.
- When the meat is browned and almost at the end of cooking, add wine and stock, depending on the recipe.
- Remove from heat once it has finished cooking.

## Poach

- Soak game meats in running water to remove any impurities.
- Bring to a boil in cold water.
- Skim.
- Add an aromatic: carrots, onions, cloves, the green part of leeks, celery, bouquet garni, garlic, and peppercorns.
- Season with coarse salt.
- Boil and skim frequently during cooking.
- Turn the heat down to very low.
- Once cooked, remove the poached item from the broth.

## Roast

- Start with a hot oven.
- Brown all sides of the meat.
- Then, lower the heat in the oven.
- Baste frequently while the meat is cooking.
- Once the cooking time is reached, remove the meat from the roasting pan.
- Place the roasting pan on a burner of the stove to caramelize the meat juices.
- Skim off the fat.
- Deglaze with a small amount of brown poultry stock.
- Reduce for a few minutes.
- Strain the jus through a cone-shaped sieve.

## Sauté

- Put some oil into a sauté pan and heat.
- Put food into the hot oil, skin side down.
- Brown the food depending on the recipe.
- Turn it as soon as soon as it browns.
- Cover and cook on low heat.
- Remove the food that is done.
- Finish cooking the larger pieces of food.
- Remove all the cooked food.
- Take the time to skim the fat off well.
- Deglaze with wine (depending on the recipe).
- Reduce slowly.
- Add the stock (depending on the recipe).
- Reduce for a few minutes.
- Adjust the seasoning.
- Strain through a cone-shaped sieve.

# Butchering Techniques
## Preparing Flounder Roulades

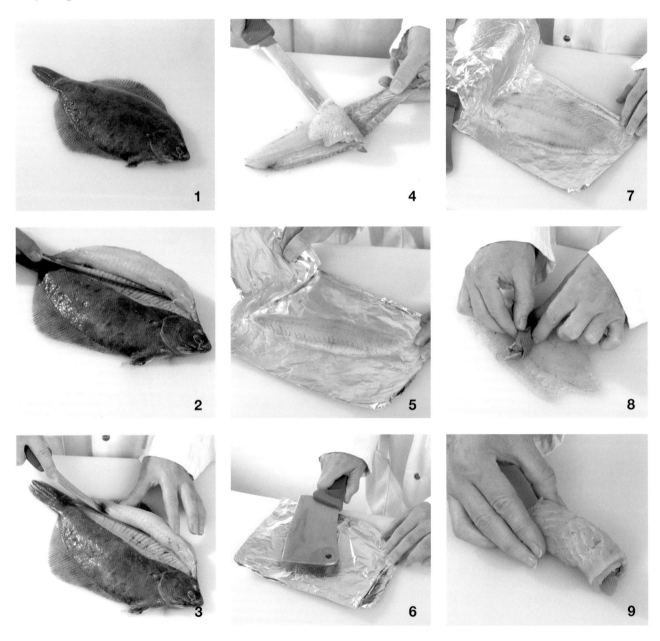

## How to Stuff Supremes (Breasts)

1

2

3

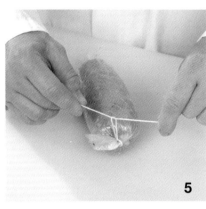

4

5

## How to Remove Bitterness from Endives

1

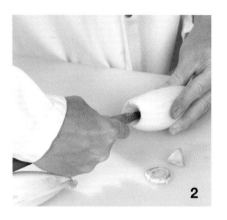

2

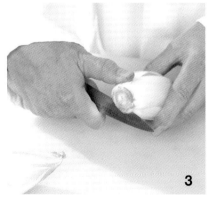

3

# Butterflying a Duck

# How to Debone a Quail

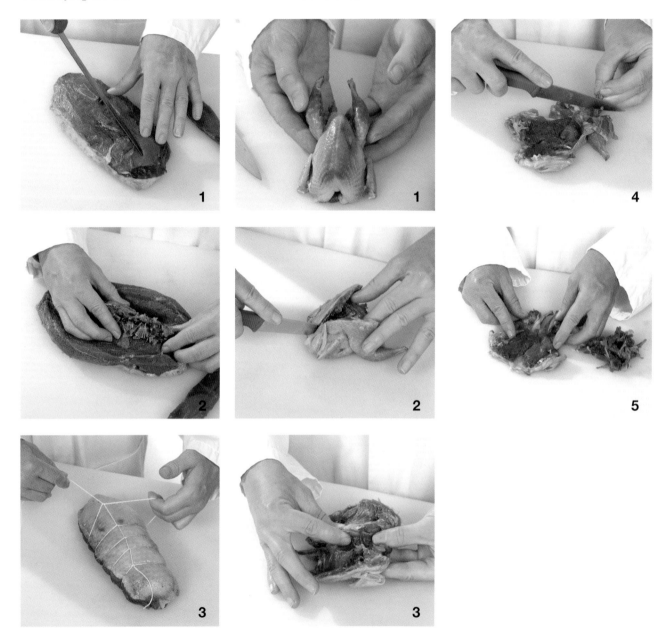

1

1

4

2

2

5

3

3

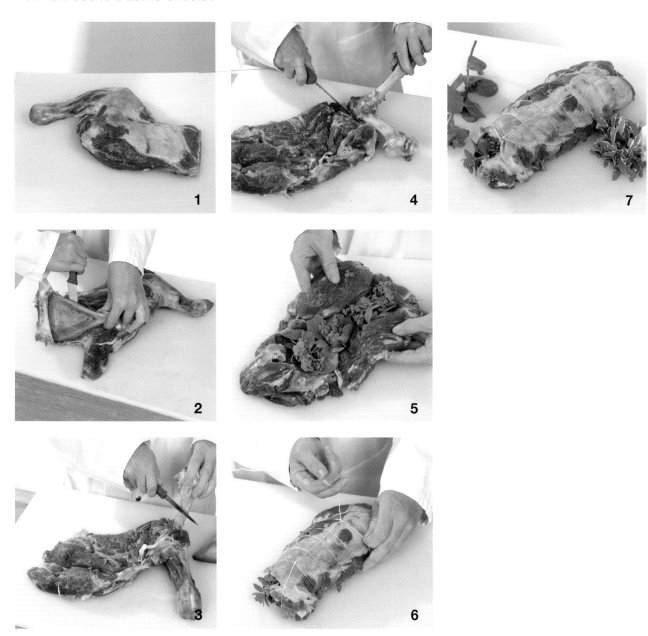

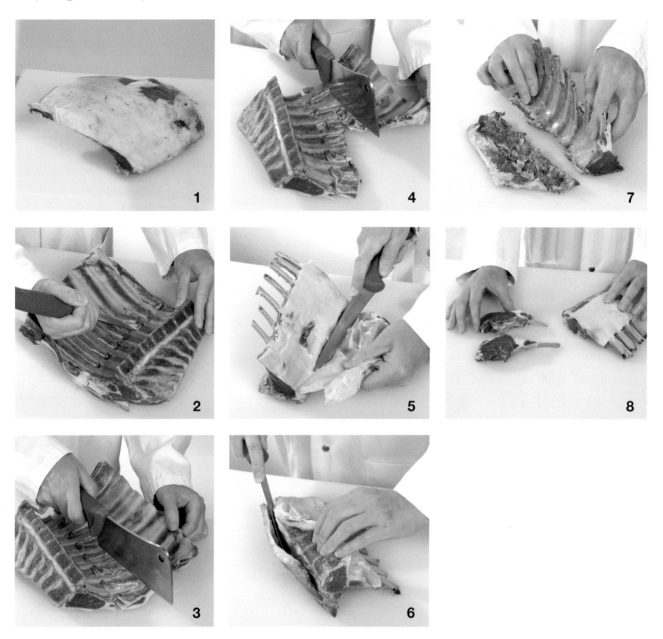

# Glossary

## "À GOUTTE DE SANG"

Literally: "To a drop of blood." When poultry or game bird breasts are cooked until just done, pierce with a skewer. A drop of blood should pearl in the centre of the fat.

## AROMATIC

All parts of an herb, plant, or root that release a pleasant fragrance.

## BLANC DE CUISSON

Mixture of water and flour added to lemon juice or white vinegar.

## BLANCH

Boiling food in a specific amount of liquid for a brief period of time to remove impurities or to tenderize.

## BOUQUET GARNI

Aromatic ingredient composed of celery, thyme sprigs, parsley, and bay leaves tied together in a bunch. It gives a pleasing flavour to dishes.

## BRAISE

To cook in a small amount of liquid in a Dutch oven or a pot with an airtight lid. Since this method of cooking takes a long time, use good, airtight pots and pans to prevent the cooking liquid from evaporating.

## BREADCRUMBS or BREADING

Stale bread crust put through a food mill or processor and dried. Fresh sliced bread with no crusts can also be used.

## BROWN

To quickly sauté meat (or vegetables) to turn the surface brown before adding a liquid (different from searing, which is meant to char the meat).

## "BRUNOISE" or DICE

Vegetables are first julienned, then cut into small cubes measuring about 3 mm.

## CHERVIL SPRIG

Chervil that has been freshly picked.

## COAT

To coat or cover hot or cold food with sauce or jelly.

## DEGLAZE

To dissolve the caramelized juices on the bottom of the pan with stock or liquid.

## EMULSIFY

Beat vigorously with a whisk or in a blender.

## FINISH WITH BUTTER

Dot a sauce with pieces of butter and stir until the sauce is blended.

## GASTRIQUE

Literally a sweet and sour sauce that involves adding vinegar or fruit juice to caramelized sugar, to which herbs and spices can also be added.

## GRILL

Cook food with direct heat, in an electric broiler or by direct contact with a flame, a hot stone, or a very hot cast iron grill pan.

## INTERNAL TEMPERATURE
The degree of doneness measured by a thermometer in the centre of a piece of meat.

## JULIENNE
Any food (meat or vegetable) cut into thin strips of 3 to 5 cm long and 1 to 2 mm thick.

## MACERATE
Let fruit, vegetables, or meat soak in alcohol or an aromatic liquid.

## MAGRET
The breast of a fattened duck or goose.

## MARINATE
To soak meat or poultry in a marinade to tenderize it and give it more flavour.

## MELT
In general, to cook food covered on low heat in a small amount of liquid and fat.

## MINCE
Julienne food (such as onions, lettuce, sorrel) and cut to a fine dice.

## MIREPOIX
Vegetables (usually carrot, onion, celery, and leeks) and sometimes lard or ham, diced and used as a base for a sauce or a stock.

## MOISTEN
Add liquid to a recipe. The liquid can be water, milk, stock, braising liquid, or wine. *"Mouiller à hauteur"* means to add enough liquid to just cover what you're cooking.

## PAN-FRY
Gently cook in a pan with fat or oil, seasoning, and a bit of liquid (water, stock, wine, etc.), or quickly cook thinly sliced meat.

## POACH
Cook food in any amount of liquid while maintaining a gentle simmer.

## POMME NOISETTES
Small balls of potato flesh formed with a melon baller and browned.

## POMMES PARISIENNES
Balls of potato flesh (larger than pomme noisettes) formed with a melon baller and browned.

## PREPARATION
Steps in a recipe to prepare a dish.

## REDUCE
Boil or simmer a sauce or stock to evaporate the liquid and make it stronger in flavour and richer in colour.

## ROAST
Cook meat in its own fat over an open flame or in an oven or rotisserie.

## SAUCE
Spread or pour sauce around a dish.

## SAUTÉ
Literally, to make the food "jump" in the pan so it won't stick. Cook in fat on high heat in a sauté pan or skillet while stirring constantly.

## SEAR
Cook meat in very hot fat to char the meat (different from browning, which is intended to give colour to the meat).

## SIMMER
Cook slowly on low heat.

## SLICE THINLY
Cut food or large vegetables (onions, leeks, etc.) into thin slices.

## SLOW STIRRING
To slowly stir a sauce or cream to prevent the formation of a skin, or to melt butter into a mixture.

## STEAM
Cook food in a small amount of liquid on low heat, covered.

## STUFF
Fill the inside of poultry or a piece of meat with a stuffing mixture.

## SWEAT
To cook vegetables in fat to release and concentrate their liquid.

# Herb Glossary

## ALTERATIVE
Detoxifies the bloodstream. It often works slowly with lasting results.

## ANTIDEPRESSANT
Counteracts depression.

## ANTIEMETIC
Relieves and/or reduces the frequency of nausea and vomiting.

## ANTIFUNGAL
Destroys yeasts and fungus.

## ANTIRHEUMATIC
Treats rheumatoid arthritis. A term that includes many functions such as a diuretic and an anti-inflammatory.

## ANTISCORBUTIC
Prevents or cures scurvy. Rich in vitamin C.

## ANTISEPTIC
Destroys or prevents microbial pathogen development. This term is often associated with a specific organ: pulmonary antiseptic, intestinal antiseptic.

## ANTISPASMODIC
Prevents, relieves, and calms muscular contractions.

## ANTI-GALACTAGOGUE
Reduces the production of breast milk.

## ANTITUSSIVE
Calms or inhibits coughing.

## ANTIVENIN

An antitoxin that acts against the venom of a snake, spider, or other poisonous animal or insect.

## ANTIVIRAL

Cures and controls infection from viruses.

## APERITIVE

Stimulates and encourages appetite; usually bitters or aromatics.

## ASTRINGENT

Shrinks mucous membranes and other tissues. It often contains tannins that bind with surface proteins to form a protective layer.

## ATONY

Refers to a muscle that has lost its strength or ability to contract normally. Atonic muscles can be digestive, intestinal, cardiac, uterine, etc.

## BACTERICIDAL

A substance that destroys bacteria.

## BALANCER

Modulates the nervous and hormonal systems to achieve equilibrium of bodily functions.

## CARDIAC ARRHYTHMIA

Irregular heart beat; more precisely, bradycardia (too slow) and tachycardia (too fast).

## CARDIOTONIC

Having a tonic effect on the action of the heart.

## CARMINATIVE

Facilitates expelling of intestinal gas to relieve flatulence or abdominal pain.

## CICATRIZANT

Promotes healing through the formation of scar tissue. There are many healing plants and herbs (vulnerary), such as Arnica, Calendula, Comfrey, Echinacea, etc.

## DEMULCENT

Forms a soothing (emollient) film over a mucous membrane to relieve minor pain and irritation.

## DIAPHORETIC

Opens pores in the skin and promotes perspiration.

## DIGESTIVE

Facilitates digestion by secreting gastric juices.

## DIURETIC

Augments and stimulates production and excretion of urine.

## EMMENAGOGUE

Stimulates or regulates menstruation.

## EXPECTORANT

Promotes the discharge of phlegm or mucus from the respiratory tract, usually through coughing.

## GALACTAGOGUE

Stimulates the production of milk.

## HEATING AGENT

Stimulates circulation by using spices (e.g., capsicum) to increase body temperature.

## HEMATINIC
Works against anaemia, generally by increasing the amount of haemoglobin in the blood.

## HEMOSTATIC
Stops hemorrhages and bleeding.

## HYPERTENSOR
Raises blood pressure.

## HYPOGLYCEMIC
Having an abnormally low amount of sugar (glucose) in the blood.

## IMMUNE SYSTEM TONIC
Nourishes, supports, and strengthens the immune system.

## LAXATIVE
Stimulates or promotes defecation.

## MUCOLYTIC
Loosens mucous and promotes decongestion.

## RUBEFACIANT
A medicine for external application that produces redness of the skin (such as a mustard plaster) to treat or prevent or alleviate the symptoms of disease by drawing out toxins.

## SEDATIVE
To promote relaxation and sleep.

## STIMULANT
An agent that accelerates physiological or organic activity. Stimulant is a general term, but it can also be used specifically, such as in nervous system stimulant, immune system stimulant, circulatory system stimulant, etc.

## TONIC
Nourishes, supports, energizes, and strengthens different bodily systems or organs. This term is often associated with a specific system such as immune system tonic, adrenal tonic, vascular tonic, etc.

## VASODILATATOR
An agent that relaxes or widens blood vessels to maintain or lower blood pressure.

## VERMIFUGE
Expels worms and parasites from the intestines.

# Index